The
SACRED DIARY
of
Adrian Plass
ON TOUR

Books by Adrian Plass

A Year at St Yorick's
Adrian Plass Classics
An Alien at St Wilfred's
And Jesus Will Be Born
Clearing Away the Rubbish
Colours of Survival (with Bridget Plass)
From Growing Up Pains to the Sacred Diary
Ghosts
The Heart of the Family
Never Mind the Reversing Ducks
Nothing but the Truth
The Sacred Diary of Adrian Plass, On Tour
The Sacred Diaries of Adrian, Andromeda and Leonard
Stress Family Robinson
Stress Family Robinson 2: The Birthday Party
The Visit
Why I Follow Jesus
You Say Tomato (with Paul McCusker)

The
SACRED DIARY
of
Adrian Plass
ON TOUR

Age Far Too
Much to Be Put
on the Front
Cover of a Book

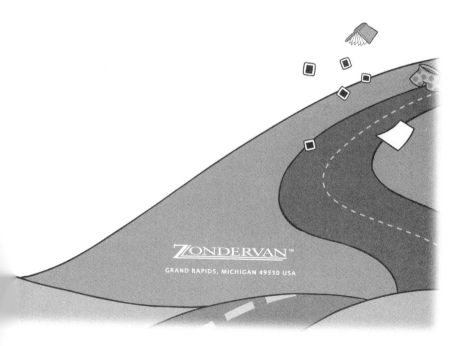

ZONDERVAN™

GRAND RAPIDS, MICHIGAN 49530 USA

ZONDERVAN™

The Sacred Diary of Adrian Plass, On Tour
Copyright © 2004 by Adrian Plass

Requests for information should be addressed to:
Zondervan, *Grand Rapids, Michigan 49530*

Adrian Plass asserts the moral right to be identified as the author of this work.

ISBN 0-007-13045-7

This edition printed on acid-free paper.

Interior design by Beth Shagene

Illustrations by Terry Workman

Printed in the United States of America

04 05 06 07 08 09 10 / ❖ DC/ 10 9 8 7 6 5 4 3 2

This book is dedicated to Ben Ecclestone,
in memory of countless miles and many fine curries

HOW IT ALL BEGAN

Anne seems to think it would be a good idea to let people see some of the diary entries I've written in connection with the little seven-day speaking tour that she and I have just done. We had a day off in the middle, so it was actually only six evening meetings with a couple of lunchtime events thrown in, but it was fun in many ways.

I wasn't sure it was interesting enough to share with others, and I suppose I might have argued with her, but there's not a lot of point really. Her track record up to the present day is one of scarily unremitting rightness as far as I'm concerned. She and God between them seem to have got Adrian Plass just where both of them want me.  Not that I'm complaining, I hasten to add. I'd rather be married to Anne than anyone else in the world, and we've been very happy together on the whole.

Mind you, not everybody would agree with that. We had a Christian couple from America staying with us for one night a few months ago. They were called Tod and Wilma Valance, and they were both very fit and large-boned and tanned with crinkly, wisely insightful smiles, deep sincere voices and huge, gleamingly white teeth. After waving them goodbye we discovered a book called *Where Is God When Marriage Falls Apart?* on our hall table. On the cover was a picture of the platonic ideal of man and woman gazing adoringly at each other. These visions bore a strong resemblance to the Valances. Inside, one of our guests had written: 'From Tod and Wilma, with agape love, and faith that the sun will rise once more on the long night of your relationship in the blessed days to come.'

Anne smiled and said, 'Oh dear, there we are, then. I suppose you and I are going to have to get a sun-ray lamp and a couple of sets of giant false-teeth. You can be called Buzz, and I'll be called Lois. What do you think?'

We laughed quite a lot over Tod and Wilma and their impressive ministry of discouragement, but I did ask Anne what she thought it could have been that made them think our marriage was on the rocks.

'Oh, well,' she said, 'they failed to realise that the quality of our marriage has risen to a level they couldn't possibly match. I mean, just consider the fact that, nowadays, we stop in the middle of a row to have coffee and a chat before carrying on. Now that's what I call progress in a relationship.'

Anyway, whatever Tod and Wilma might think, God has given both of us a happy marriage, and he's given me a wife who offers very good advice, even if I don't always want to hear it.

And I have to admit, when I think about it, that there were some special things about this tour, things that might be worth writing about. Perhaps the most special was the fact that our son, Gerald, was able to come with us and even do some of the speaking. Gerald is in his first curacy at a busy church in London, and he had been intending to be with us for a week of his holiday before we went away, and then spend a week at our house on his own during the tour.

However, we were able to afford the expenses involved in Gerald joining us because of another special thing. A new member of our church, a man we knew only by sight, who was called Barry Ingstone, was keen for his Christian printing business to sponsor our tour so that, as he put it in a letter to me, 'the gospel can be preached and souls saved for God in these, our times'. I suppose the last bit meant 'now'. The idea was that he would guarantee the costs of the tour, and we would give him whatever we made from gifts or ticket sales. He would make sure that any difference was covered.

I have to be honest and say that, important though this aim was, the first thing to cross my mind on reading these words had nothing to do with Gerald. It was the purely selfish, deeply wonderful possibility that we wouldn't have to stay with people! If the funding was sufficient we would be able to stay in Guest Houses and small hotels on all of the seven nights, apart from one in the middle when we were going to be close enough to come home in the early morning and have a day and a night off.

So very relieved!

I ought to explain that my experiences of staying in people's houses when I go to speak at their churches has been – well,

variable, to say the least. Some are wonderful. Lots are not. Anne's much better at it than I am. She says I make an enormous fuss about things that are quite simple really. Well, maybe I do, but that's because they worry me so much.

Take the whole business of having to use *alien* bathrooms in the morning. I just can't stand it. I really can't.

I remember staying the night up north, for instance, with a family called Davenport. They were nice people. I'm sure they were very nice people, but – well, they were so much not *my* family, if you understand what I mean.

I knew, because I'd learned it the evening before, that there were only three people staying in the house apart from myself. There was the father, Geoff Davenport, bluff, good-natured and keen that I should treat his home as if it was my own and just do exactly as I wished. There was the mother, Vera Davenport, smart, efficient and very insistent that I should relax, as long, I suspected, as I didn't damage or mess up anything in her incredibly clean and well-organised house. And there was the daughter, Sally Davenport, a bright, pretty girl of about fourteen, far too busy in her own head to do more than vaguely register anyone else's existence, let alone mine. She appeared to agree more or less politely with everything I said but otherwise volunteered nothing. Just three people. Three of them. That's all there were. I swear it.

When I woke up on the morning after my talk in the Davenports' near-perfect spare room, I lay still for a minute just listening. Glancing at the ornate guest alarm clock beside me I saw that it was only seven o'clock. There was one of those profound, ticking hushes throughout the house.

Great!

Climbing swiftly out of bed making as little noise as possible, I congratulated myself on having woken before anyone else. If I was quick I could get into the bathroom, have my shower and be safely back in the bedroom before any of the other three had even got up. I swiftly scanned the mental map of the rooms along the landing that I had drawn the night before. To my left were two rooms, one a second spare room, and the other Geoff and Vera's room, and to my right were the bathroom and Sally's bedroom.

Essential to get that part of my forthcoming journey right, I told myself tensely. Creeping on tiptoe into the bedroom occupied by my host's teenage daughter dressed only in a towel at seven o'clock in the morning might fall just outside the terms of Geoff's genial suggestion that I should feel free to do just exactly as I wished.

I had actually turned the handle of my bedroom door and was opening it a millimetre at a time with enormous, tongue-protruding concentration when I heard the thunderous sound of Geoff and Vera's bedroom door opening.

Clenched my teeth and closed my own door as silently as possible, then scuttled back to the safety of my bed in terror. Meeting people I barely know on strange landings in ablution mode is just about the pits as far as I'm concerned.

Sat miserably on the bed and made a clear-headed, sensible policy decision. Right, I said to myself, one person is clearly on his or her way to use the bathroom. When they've finished there'll be another two. Bearing this in mind, I'm simply going to sit tight here on my bed and wait until all the other occupants of the house have finished their showering and teeth cleaning and whatever else they do in the mornings, and then, when there's no doubt that all three have gone downstairs and left the coast clear – it will be my turn. Easy on the face of it.

But that's when it began. The endless, inexplicable, unremitting traffic of human beings from one end of the corridor to the other and back again. It was as if, in the wake of some huge natural disaster in Geoff and Vera's room, vast numbers of refugees were obliged, one by one, to make the trek along the landing to the safety of the bathroom. When that flow eased, and I was just beginning to think that my time might be coming after all, they started coming out of Sally's room, one after another, to and fro, hordes of them, tramping into the bathroom, running water, rattling things, coughing, spluttering, tramping out again, opening and closing doors, making it impossible for me to emerge. As far as I could tell, the landing just outside my door was a seething, surging mass of unwashed and washed humanity, incomprehensibly thronging a house that had seemed to have only three people living in it the night before.

Just as I was resigning myself to the rest of my life being spent in the spare bedroom, there was an abrupt silence, followed by a tentative tap on my door.

'Bathroom's free-e-e!' fluted Vera Davenport, in her calling-out-to-a-guest voice.

'Oh, good, right, thanks!' I gurgled back.

Wary of a trick, I opened my door with meticulous care and looked both ways along the landing. Nobody in sight. The refugees and all the other hordes had gone. Taut with apprehension I began my journey towards the end of the corridor and was actually on the point of arrival when the bedroom door immediately beside me began to open and I flung myself with a tiny scream into the bathroom, slamming the door behind me and bolting it on the inside.

Having recovered sufficiently to look around, I made the unnerving discovery that, as I had feared, the Davenport bathroom was perfect. It was bound to be, wasn't it? That bathroom sparkled with little points of light. It gleamed. It shone smugly at me. It silently challenged me to do anything that would not result in it becoming less clean and less hygienic than it had been before I started. There was only one direction for this showplace to go, and that was down. Vera Davenport must have been in here after the other fifteen thousand members of her family had finished, wiping and polishing and spraying away any polluting traces of human activity that they might have left. I tried to photograph the room with my mind before I showered, anxious that everything should be left as I'd found it. After finishing I cleaned every surface I could remember touching like a dervish, knowing, even as I scrubbed, that, however hard I worked, one indisputable fact must remain – this bathroom would be less perfect when I left it than when I had entered.

When I got home after that trip and told Anne what had happened, she laughed and said that I needed to separate out my problems from other people's. If Vera Davenport wanted to have a bathroom that looked as if it had never been used, that was her problem, not mine. If I didn't like creeping around other people's houses in the early morning that was my problem, not theirs.

I agreed with her and felt very silly when I thought of me cleaning away feverishly in that bathroom, trying to keep it up to some impossible standard that was no real use to anyone anyway. Next time I do stay with people I am resolved to be far more adult and assertive about the whole thing.

In the meantime, I was *so glad* we were going to be able to stay in hotels!

Having said all that, I had more or less accepted Barry Ingstone's offer before being informed of a seriously complicating factor. He was intending to come with us!

When we met one Saturday afternoon to discuss the tour, Barry began by stunning Anne and me with the magnitude of his offer. Looking rather like a shaved and sedated Ben Elton he explained, with somewhat surprisingly frequent references to verses from the Bible, that he was prepared to finance travel arrangements in the form of a rented vehicle together with all expenses, and accommodation for up to six people – *six!* – depending on how large my 'team' was.

Of course, I hadn't actually got a 'team' as such, but, catching Anne's eye, I decided on the spot that Gerald and Leonard Thynn were essential to the task in hand. We always love having Gerald with us, and Leonard gets so lonely when we're both away. I felt quite greedy. Tentatively, I pointed out to Barry that, if the budget allowed for it, we would love to take a back-projector and screen so that we could show slides. There were points in the talks I was planning where it would be very useful to have certain images appearing on a large screen, but quite apart from simply adding another dimension to our evenings, there was a particular reason for putting this suggestion forward.

Old Zak Chambers, a member of our church who died in his mid-eighties only last year, used to be a professional painter. He turned out meticulous water-colours of country churches

15

and old mills and that sort of thing, and, as far as I know, sold everything he did. When Zak had a serious stroke three years ago he was confined to a wheelchair and lost the use of his right hand. I suppose we all automatically assumed that the painting would have to stop.

It didn't.

As Zak's devoted but very straightforward wife Bernadette has always said, he was a stubborn old git. He painstakingly taught himself to paint with his left hand, and the results were – well, they were extraordinary. It was as if the old man had found a new kind of freedom right at the end of his painting career. He mostly painted the hills that could be seen swelling up in the distance when you sat down at the end of his back garden, but the interesting thing was that his new, left-handed style was a lifetime away from the old one. These pictures were not exactly abstracts, but they seemed to be alive with light and movement and, as Edwin our elder put it, exciting possibilities. They simply glowed with the old fellow's love for the natural world. He really played with paint when he did those. Getting ready for heaven, Anne said.

I had already thought how marvellous it would be to take some slides of Zak's later pictures and use them to accompany poems and Bible-readings and that sort of thing. If Barry was serious about the money, this was an ideal chance to do it. Apart from anything else, if Bernadette agreed, we could take some of the originals with us and exhibit them for sale at the venues. Zak's widow was reasonably well off, so she didn't need the money, but I knew she would love to feel that her beloved husband's pictures were being appreciated and that some of them might go to good homes, as it were.

I explained all this to Barry and pointed out that if Leonard came, he would be able to take responsibility for erecting the screen and showing the slides at each of the venues.

Throwing a few more chunks of scripture out like shrapnel, Barry intimated that this would not be a problem. I shook hands with him, inwardly hugging to myself the excitement of being able to do things 'properly' for once.

It was then that Barry dropped his bombshell.

He was coming with us!

He wanted to be part of the joy of outreach, he said, and see for himself how the bread he was casting upon the waters would return to him during and after the seven days of our tour.

Well, of course, we agreed. What else could we do? What would you have done? To coin a less biblical but equally applicable saying, Barry was the piper and was therefore entitled to play any tune he jolly well liked. So we agreed.

I think, deep down, my main worry was not so much that Barry was so addicted to scripture quotation, irksome though that habit was likely to become, but a fear of what would happen when Gerald encountered him. You never know what my son is going to do or say when it comes to people like Barry. We just prayed that it would all be all right.

I popped round to see Bernadette that same day to ask how she felt about my plan. 'Tickled pink' just about sums up her response. I think she would have insisted on coming with us if she'd been ten years younger. We spent a very enjoyable couple of hours going through the paintings and working out how much to charge the folks who might 'adopt' them. Bernadette said that her semi-professional photographer grandson would do the slides for us, so that was that.

Of course, when Leonard heard about all this he was wildly overjoyed at the prospect of joining us for another tour and became quite foolishly brash and confident about the ease with which he would be able to handle the back-projector and slides that we were planning to hire. As you will see later this confidence may have been just a little premature.

It was, incidentally, in connection with Leonard that yet another very special thing happened, and it resulted in one other person being added to my 'team'. Her name was – but no, this is a good place to begin sharing my diary extracts with you. Our tour was due to begin on the twenty-first of September, and the first entry comes exactly one week before that, on the Friday. Gerald had arrived by the time the second of these entries was made, and as usual it was as though he'd never been away.

FRIDAY, 14 SEPTEMBER

Have just had a staggering phone call at work this morning from Leonard Thynn. He tells me he has a girlfriend! Amazing! Asked him what her name was.

'She's called Angels Twitten,' said Leonard, sounding more excited than I've heard him for a long time, 'so if we get married I'll be called Leonard Twitten, won't I?'

'No, Leonard, the woman is usually called by the man's name, so after you got married she'd be – '

'Leonard Twitten?'

'No, the woman keeps her first name but takes the man's second name. Do you see what I mean?'

'Oh, I see. I didn't know that. Yes, I understand.'

Short pause while the wheels silently turned.

'Adrian, I do understand, but – how am I going to manage without a second name?'

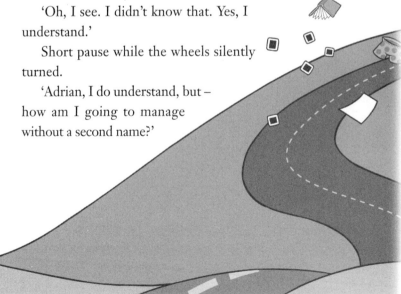

Gripped the telephone more tightly.

'No, Leonard, you haven't understood at all, have you? You *keep* your second name.'

'But you just said the woman takes it.'

'I know I did, but I didn't mean – look, isn't it a bit early to be talking about marriage, Leonard. You can't have known this lady for very long. Have you been out on – you know – dates and things?'

'Oh, yes, we had a big night out last night.'

'Where did you go – somewhere special?'

'Yes, we had a very nice evening indeed, thank you. We took the bus up to Tesco's to watch the videos.'

'Really? I know they've got a café at Tesco's. I didn't know you could watch videos there.'

'Oh, yes, there were two good ones on last night. There was one really excellent one at the end of the household cleaning aisle about a new kind of squeezy-mop that absorbs twice as much dirty water because of a revolutionary new type of sponge that's bigger than usual when it's dry but much, much smaller when it's wet.'

'Leonard – '

'We saw that one three times. My favourite bit is when the lady lifts the end of the mop up and looks at it as if she can't believe how much water it's soaked up, and Angels' best bit is when the lady's little girl comes in and says, "Gosh, Mummy, how did you get our floor so sparkling clean," and the lady looks at her and says, "By using the new Miracle Mop, darling, it's cut my floor-cleaning time in half." And the other one – '

'Leonard – '

'The other one is one we'd both seen before in the middle of the Kitchen and Household aisle about a special plastic thing that cuts fruit and vegetables into all sorts of different shapes just by adding a different plastic thing to the plastic thing that you hold, tomatoes in star-shapes and things like that. Oh, and there's a really good bit near the end – well, it's not as good if you know it's coming, like we did, but it really takes you by surprise the first time you see it, and it's fun watching other people's faces who haven't seen it before – when the man looks as if he's finished, and then he suddenly says, "Of course, the Magic Multi-cutter can't do your chips for you, can it? That would be far too much to expect. Sure about that? Just you watch this!"'

'Leonard – '

'And then, just as you're thinking, no, it's not possible – if you've not seen it before, I mean – he puts a new plastic thing on the other plastic thing, gets a big potato, and before you know it there's a pile of chips on the table, and you know then that the Magic Multi-cutter *can* do your chips for you! You feel like clapping!'

'But you don't actually clap, do you Leonard? Tell me you and Angels didn't clap at the end of the video.'

'Oh, come *on*, Adrian!' said Leonard, 'Tsk! Tsk! Tsk!' He tutted away as if I'd made some terminally foolish suggestion. 'It's a supermarket, not a theatre. You don't clap in supermarkets, do you, not unless you're an idiot?'

'No,' I said, 'sorry, Leonard – silly me, I don't know what I was thinking of. So, Angels is quite happy to go out to the supermarket for the evening. She doesn't fancy the cinema or a restaurant or something like that?'

'Well, we only had enough money for the bus, and anyway we like Tesco's because that's where we first met. Last night was our tenth anniversary.'

'What! Ten years? Why have you never told us about her before?'

'Ten days,' said Leonard, 'and fifteen hours and twenty-four minutes. I'm a bit vague about the seconds. Yes, we met at six o'clock on a Tuesday evening in the wines and spirits aisle of Tesco's. I've been asking God to find me a girlfriend for ages, but I was a bit nervous, so I always said could he choose someone I'd got some big thing in common with. Well, he did. It's great! We're both recovering alcoholics.'

'You're both – '

'And on the day we met we both thought exactly the same things. We were standing next to each other looking at all the different kinds of whisky and thinking, "That's what I want most!" And then it was like one of those videos – not the mop and vegetable ones, I don't mean. I mean the ones you don't get round to seeing at the cinema because it costs too much. We turned and looked at each other and – don't know how to say it, Adrian – at exactly the same moment we saw something we might want even more. It was like magic. Not magic, I don't mean. I mean – you know – magic. Can I bring her round tomorrow evening to meet you and Anne? I've told her you're my best friends.'

Could hardly speak.

'Yes, of course you can, Leonard. We'd love to meet Angels. Come at seven o'clock and we'll have a meal together.'

'Okay. By the way, I haven't told her that I'm a Christian. Don't want to spoil everything. So we won't mention that, eh? Bye!'

Oh, dear . . .

SATURDAY, 15 SEPTEMBER

Such a treat to have Gerald arrive home this morning. He still tends to treat me as if I was a very confused ninety-three-year-old, but we love him dearly. Wonderful to see him! I still find it hard to believe that this separate, grown-up, competent person is *my* son. He said how much he was enjoying the prospect of the tour, and how good it would be for me to have him and Anne to be there making sure my feet stayed firmly on the ground. Anne nodded agreement. Hmm . . .

He also offered to do a bit of speaking if I wanted him to and said that he'd got a few pieces prepared if we wanted him to use them. Excellent! We've never really heard Gerald speak publicly before, not properly anyway, but with a mind like his it would have to be interesting whatever it was. We spent the afternoon going over plans for some of the speaking engagements.

All three of us got quite childishly excited this evening waiting for Leonard to turn up with his girlfriend. Lots of speculation from Gerald and me about her looks, how old she would be and the way in which Leonard was likely to conduct a relationship. Anne said we must forget about anything Leonard said to me about her over the phone and just greet her as a friend of a good friend. Gerald said he was ever so glad that Leonard had found a girl-friend and deeply intrigued by the idea of him 'turning into a couple'.

'Strange name, though, isn't it?' he said. 'Angels Twitten. I've never heard of anyone called Angels before.'

Doorbell went at exactly seven o'clock. Opened the door to find a lady I'd never seen before standing alone on the step. She was in her mid-thirties, shortish, slim and quite pretty, but with big sad eyes and dressed in rather vividly coloured, drifty, hippyish clothes. Her frizzy, dark-brown hair was pushed back in a headband, decorated with lots of little blue plastic flowers. She was holding a bottle of milk with a crumpled top in one hand. Soft, beautiful voice, nervous but full of resonance.

She said, 'Hello, my name is Angels Twitten, and I've come to dinner with my fiancé, Leonard Thynn.'

'Right! Very pleased to meet you, Angels. Do come in. Er, when you say you've come *with* Leonard, he doesn't seem actually to be er – '

Interrupted by the phone ringing just as I'd ushered her into the hall and closed the door. It was Thynn. Well, of *course* it was.

'Hello, Adrian, I'm speaking from that phone-box next to the Salvation Army Citadel up at the top end of town.'

'But why – '

'I'm ringing to apologise for being late.'

'But you're not late. At least, Angels isn't late. It's seven o'clock now and she's already here. I've just let her in.'

'Oh, good, I'm glad. Yes, I was with her just now in the next street down from yours. The thing is, I will be late by the time I get back from here.'

'Yes, but why did you go all the way up to the citadel?'

'To find a phone that worked.'

Aware that the familiar headache was beginning.

'So why didn't you just come in and use our phone?'

'Because it was you I wanted to call.'

Felt like screaming.

'But if you wanted to speak to me, why didn't you just come in and talk to me?'

'Because we were early. We were waiting round the corner for it to be time. Then I thought it would be a good idea to ring you to ask if we could come in a bit early, but the nearest phone had been vandalised and there was a queue for the next one, and by the time I managed to find a phone that was free and working I was so far away that it was too late to be early, so there was no point in phoning to ask about coming early, but it was too late to get back to your house without being late, so in the end I decided to ring to apologise for how late I'm going to be by the time I get back to your house.'

!

'Leonard! You've never ever worried about being early or late or coming on the off-chance or not turning up at all in the past. Why on earth should we mind if you come a few minutes early this evening?'

Short pause.

'Well, you know. It's different because of – you know, because of . . .'

25

Sighed, and said weakly, 'All right, Leonard, don't worry about being late. Just come back now as quickly as you can and everything will be fine. See you in a few minutes.'

Put the phone down and turned to find Angels holding the bottle of milk towards me.

'For you and Anne,' she said.

I said, 'Oh, thank you. Did we leave it on the step?'

'No, Leonard wanted us to bring a bottle as it was a dinner party, but we'd only got half a bottle of milk each and no money to get anything else, so we poured it all into one bottle and put the top back on. I thought it was a bit of a funny thing to bring, but Leonard said you really liked milk, so . . .'

'Ah, yes, of course, thank you. A bottle of milk. How nice. Leonard's absolutely right. We love milk. Thank you *very* much . . .'

Ten minutes later all was as it should have been. Leonard (rather nervous) sitting next to Angels on the sofa as if they were both being interviewed for a job. Angels seems a funny mixture of all sorts of things. Bright, confident, ill at ease, vague, practical, dreamy.

After all eating in an unusually well-mannered way we settled in the sitting-room again and Gerald said, 'Angels, I hope you don't mind me asking, but I was wondering about your name. I mean, Angels is quite unusual, isn't it? In fact, come to think of it, I can't remember ever hearing of anyone with your surname either. Were you christened Angels Twitten?'

'I don't mind you asking at all,' said Angels solemnly, fixing her big, dark eyes on Gerald. 'I was actually christened Angela

26

Pathway, but my father had a very bad time at school when he was a boy because some of the others nicknamed him "Doggy Paradise" and he didn't want my brother and I to go through that so he changed his name to "Twitten", which is a word they use down in Kent for a narrow alley way that connects one area of housing to another. And I changed my name from Angela to Angels because a man at the council put his finger on the wrong key when he wrote to me and when I saw it I rather liked it, so I decided I would be Angels from then on.'

'Ah, yes, of course,' nodded Gerald, smiling, 'the "a" and the "s" are next door to each other, aren't they? Well, I think you were quite right. Angels is much nicer than Angela. But how did you get on at school with "Twitten"?'

'Really awful!' Angels suddenly smiled. 'It all sounds rather silly, doesn't it?'

'No sillier than the things most parents do,' said Gerald, glancing at me for some reason.

'Angels writes poems,' said Thynn proudly, 'I made her bring one to read tonight.'

Statutory chorus of delight and encouragement. Joined in naturally, out of politeness, but personally my stomach always sinks when someone says they're going to read one of their own poems. What usually happens is that either I find what they read impenetrable, and I haven't the faintest idea whether it's good-impenetrable or bad-impenetrable, or it's just plain awful, and I have all the strain of trying to think of something to say that won't upset them, but will put them off the idea of reading the other thirteen that they just happen to have with them. Braced myself.

Angels took a folded sheet of paper from her bag. A half-sleepy, distant look came into her eyes.

'This one's not really finished,' she said apologetically, 'nothing I do is ever really finished, but I'll read it to you. It's called "Rainbow".'

I've copied it out.

> With brazen modesty
> Sumptuous simplicity
> Unique normality
> We who fly with feet upon the ground
> Are plunged headlong into the vaulting sea
> Raised to fathomless depths of calm unsettled skies
> Crudely caressed by monstrous beauty
> Captured in the freedom of obscuring light
> The selfish gift of midnight suns
> Burned with ice
> Betrayed by loyalty
> Unfettered in our chains
> Shaken from the core
> Blistered by the shade
> We, the single ragged rich who lie in state
> Yearn for unfulfillment
> And the vibrancy of death
> Curse with joy the crashing silence
> Into which we have been tragically, fatally born
> Sacredly profane
> Anciently refreshing
> Tediously new
> Such gargantuan minutiae
> Golden edged and dull
> Retreat towards us through the all revealing mist

> Until the rainbow, like a dream of war
> Glorious in monochrome
> Comes arcing, like the straightest arrow made by man
> Invisibly
> Into view.

A sort of echoing, puzzled silence descended after Angels finished reading.

Heard Gerald murmur under his breath, 'Retreat towards us? Unfettered in our chains? Sacredly profane? Hmm . . .'

Decided this was definitely one of the impenetrable variety of poems, probably impenetrable-bad, because, as Gerald said later, it seemed to be based on a sort of verbal conjuring trick where you make a long list of pairs of things that don't belong together and then put them together anyway. On the other hand, the whole thing had a sort of grand ring about it. Quite a puzzle really. Asked Anne afterwards what she thought. She said it had sounded to her like the work of someone very clever whose brain had got scrambled by too much of something that wasn't very good for her. Asked if I'd noticed how, most of the time, Angels was chatty and normal and smiley, but whenever she started talking about anything to do with the arts or any other abstract subject she seemed to go off into another world that didn't make a lot of sense. Thought about this and realised she was right. Later on in the evening, for instance, Leonard had made another announcement about his new friend.

'Angels is a dancer, aren't you, Angels?'

'Well, yes, that's what I – what I do.'

'Oh, *really*!' said Anne. 'How interesting. We know next to nothing about that. So, if you don't mind me asking, what does dance mean to you, then, Angels?'

Similar far-off look came into her eyes, but there was something else there as well, a fear and an intensity. As she spoke she waved her fingers elegantly, but as the words came out of her mouth they were like dead leaves drifting randomly on the breeze.

'What does it mean? Well, for me dance is, in essence, about assessing the philosophical parameters of a specific creative process and then being brave enough to bridge them with artistically coherent lines of communication. I see it as a fundamental realignment of spiritual force, interlocking with the vision of a specific other, or within the landscape of one's own selective imagery. It's important for the dancer to feel both the flow and undercurrent of the human heart as a maker of waves and tides across the ocean of human experience. In artistic terms, that's what dance means to me.'

Another of those echoing silences, and then Thynn said, 'So it's not about moving your legs around in patterns?'

Opening her eyes wide again, Angels nodded and gazed at him adoringly.

'Yes, Leonard, that's a very good way of putting it. You are a man of real insight.'

'*Am* I?' said Leonard, looking surprised and very pleased, 'I'd always understood from almost everyone I know that I definitely wasn't. My old headmaster told me that I was the most inchoate remnant of Neanderthal incomprehension that it had ever been his misfortune to encounter.'

He smiled with a certain wild-eyed pride.

'I learned what he thought of me by heart without trying when he made me write it out a hundred times after getting little white bits at the corner of his mouth because he wasn't able to teach me something about a bath that was "x" inches deep filling up in "y" hours when "z" amount of water came out every some other letter that I can't remember minutes.'

'You know, this is marvellous,' said Anne. 'We could do with a dancer for our tour, couldn't we, Adrian, especially now that Barry's made such a generous offer?'

'Er, yes – yes, we could.'

Tried not to let Anne see how alarmed I was by this half-suggestion. I've learned to trust my wife's instincts, but the truth is that I never have got on very well with dancers in the church at the best of times. All they seem to do is dress up in clothes that stop you from seeing any movements they make or what sex they are, and they use one of about four different ways to point upwards in a supplicating sort of way and gaze adoringly at the lampshades with one knee in the air. Besides, couldn't help thinking that if Angels' dancing turned out to be like her poetry she would probably be into moving forward at the same time as moving backwards, and throwing herself into the air in the same instant that she dropped to the floor. In the case of Angels it wasn't even as if we were likely to have a chance to see her dancing before the tour began.

'So, Angels,' asked Anne, as if she had read the last thought in my mind, 'is there anywhere we could come and watch you dancing in the very near future?'

Angels looked at the floor. Her voice seemed smaller.

'I haven't done much for a long time. It's been difficult. I am going to do something for the elderly people at Clay House tomorrow afternoon, though. It's nothing much, but I suppose if you really wanted . . .'

Arranged to go along tomorrow afternoon to watch.

'By the way,' said Angels, 'what sort of tour is it you're going on?'

Thynn turned white and looked imploringly at Anne and me.

'It's a Christian tour,' said Anne pleasantly but firmly. 'We're Christians. Adrian writes Christian books that people find – well, they find them quite funny as well as being helpful sometimes. The tour's a chance to go and tell people more about Jesus.'

'I see,' said Angels. She looked a little worried, then turned to Leonard. 'So are you a Christian as well, Leonard?'

'Sometimes,' said Thynn miserably, 'but not really – well, yes, I suppose I am.' Suddenly panicking. 'But I could easily stop if that means you won't like me any more! I don't mind what I am, honestly! What are you? I'll be one as well.'

'Why didn't you tell me?' asked Angels, 'I'm glad you're one. I expect that's what helps to make you such a good person.'

Watched relief, confusion and embarrassment chase each other across Thynn's features.

'And how about you, Angels,' said Anne, 'do you have any kind of belief?'

That distant look.

'I believe in a sacred responsibility to reach out and receive the touch of otherness, and I think we should always strive to celebrate the ethereal strands that are woven into true humanness.'

'A Methodist, then,' said Gerald.

All laughed, Angels no less than the rest of us.

Asked Anne in bed tonight what she thought about Angels.

'I like her very much,' she said, 'and I love seeing Leonard so happy. I think she's been through very tough times and has trouble facing some things. We need to make her part of us, don't you think? She might be just what we need to add something different to our tour. Let's wait and see what happens tomorrow.'

Hmm! I like Angels too. Can't help feeling a bit worried, though, that the 'philosophical parameters of a specific creative process' might boil down to a bit of wafty swaying about. We shall see.

SUNDAY, 16 SEPTEMBER

Anne and Gerald and I up to Clay House this afternoon to watch Angels after phoning to check that it would be all right. The person in charge said it would be fine. Her ladies and gentlemen loved having new faces around, she told us, but we must be prepared for them to say and do some slightly strange things because a lot of them were very confused indeed.

'Like Aunt Felicity at the Eight Bells,' said Anne when I told her.

Felt a little bit nervous after being reminded of our trips in the old days to the Eight Bells Home for Maritime Relicts. Aunt Felicity, long gone now, bless her soul, was stubbornly convinced that I had died some years ago, and seemed to feel that the way I looked when Anne and I visited was final confirmation of that deeply held belief. On one occasion, while I was present in the room and actually standing right in front of her, she strongly advised Anne to get me cremated before I started to smell.

Clay House turned out to be pleasantly friendly and cheerful on the inside, although some of the elderly folk we met today made me feel a little sad. We were confronted just on the other side of the carefully locked front door by a rosy-cheeked lady who must have been in her late eighties or early nineties. She was clutching an equally ancient looking teddy-bear under one arm.

'Hello,' she said, in a friendly, slightly anxious voice, 'my name's Elizabeth. I'm just waiting here for my mummy and daddy. They're coming to collect me soon to take me home.'

'Oh, that'll be nice, won't it?' said Anne. 'But are you going to come and watch the dancing first, Elizabeth?'

Like a little child, Elizabeth took Anne's hand, and we made our way down a long, wide corridor to a big bright, rectangular sitting-room with twenty or thirty residents sitting in armchairs arranged round the edge. At one side of the room, near a hatch that went through into a little kitchen area, Angels was kneeling on the floor doing something with a portable CD player. As we came in she looked up and saw us. She waved, flushed a little and smiled, then turned back to sorting her music out.

A few minutes later Mrs Banyon, the lady I had spoken to on the telephone, stood up and clapped her hands to attract attention.

'Well, ladies and gentlemen,' she said briskly, 'what a treat we have this afternoon. Angels Twitten is here to dance for us – you all remember Angels, don't you? She's been to see us before.'

Murmurs of agreement and a few smiles from some of the elderly residents in response to this question, but quite a few of them continued to rock or stare or sleep, while one very bent little man with deep frown lines etched onto his face made a tottering break for it towards the door, muttering grumpily that he hated 'bloody dancing' as he went. He was gently steered back to his seat by two of the care-workers. They were very nice to him, but I couldn't help feeling a bit sorry for the old man.

'And,' went on Mrs Banyon, 'we have two other visitors with us, Adrian and Anne Plass, who are friends of Angels', and we're very pleased to see them, aren't we?'

More murmurs, smiles and a few grunts, then it was time for Angels to dance.

I was dreading it by now. And I couldn't help feeling cross with Anne for mentioning the tour before we'd even seen Angels dance. If, as I suspected and feared, her 'artistic expression' turned out to be really affected and poor, it would all be terribly embarrassing. We would somehow have to not mention the tour any more, and she would know perfectly well why that was and the whole thing would get all tense and awkward. As the music started and Angels took up a starting position in the centre of the room my heart was heavy.

She was superb.

The first piece of music that she danced to was a staccato orchestral piece featuring a choir whose combined voices seemed to have the function of an extra musical instrument. There was an urgent, racing feel to the piece, and an edge of slight hysteria that made it exciting and dangerous. Angels began with slow exploratory movements, as though she was

reaching out and searching for the source of the music, eventually speeding up and moving outwards and back to the centre again, as if gradually becoming aware that the source was inside herself. Each movement, slow or rapid, was so concentrated and focused that I found myself breathlessly, almost painfully wanting to be part of what was happening to the dancer. It was a story. It was very clever, and very strong, and very full of feeling.

I don't know what was going on inside the minds of the old people who ringed the room, but there was no doubt that most of them were, at the very least, distracted and absorbed by what they were seeing and hearing. In the seat beside me Elizabeth had sat without moving during the dance, but once it had ended she turned amid the patter of applause and beckoned with her finger for me to put my ear close to her mouth.

'My daddy's a doctor,' she said, 'and he'll be home soon.'

Angels performed three more dances, each one as concentrated and fascinating as the first. I expect, knowing that we'd be there, she'd chosen her best ones, but that's what I or anyone else would have done. Afterwards, as we enjoyed the tea and piece of cake that were supplied through the hatch, we told her how wonderful we thought she had been. She blushed again and looked very pleased.

Waving goodbye to everybody, we made our way back down the corridor to the front door, still accompanied by our new friend and her teddy-bear. As Mrs Banyon held the door open for us, carefully preventing Elizabeth from walking out at the same time, the old lady looked up into Anne's face and repeated what she had said to us when we first arrived.

'My name's Elizabeth. I'm waiting for my mummy and daddy. They're coming soon to take me home.'

Anne looked at the tired old face, criss-crossed with tiny lines like a piece of antique china, and the frail body, so slight and insubstantial that it hardly seemed possible it could sustain life.

'That will be lovely, Elizabeth,' she said, 'and I'm sure you're right. They will be coming for you very soon.'

Immensely relieved that Angels turned out to be such a marvellous performer. Anne, Gerald and I spent part of the afternoon talking about how much her dancing would add to the evenings we were planning.

'The other thing,' said Anne, 'is that one or two of Zak's slides will fit in beautifully with the dancing. I can't wait to see how that works out.'

'Not to mention the fact that Leonard will be over the moon,' said Gerald, 'being able to have his sweetheart with him instead of leaving her behind. They really are crackers about each other, aren't they?'

Asked Anne what had made her so certain that we wouldn't be disappointed.

She said, 'I'm not quite sure, except that underneath all those words that didn't mean very much I felt as if I was meeting a grown-up when I first met Angels. The trouble is that something in the part of her that has to deal with the world seems to have got scrambled by things that are not really any business of ours. You have to listen hard to hear the heart of what she is. When she started saying all those extraordinary things about what dancing meant to her I didn't listen to the words so much as watch something that was happening in her eyes.'

I nodded. Even I had noticed a sort of shining in Angels when she was talking about dancing.

'I suppose,' went on Anne, 'the truth is that I could *feel* real dance resonating inside her. Does that sound very silly?'

'No, of course not, but I'm still surprised that you said anything about the tour on that first evening. I actually felt a bit cross. I mean, we hadn't had a chance to talk about it, and Leonard and Angels might have ended up terribly hurt and disappointed. Wasn't it a bit of a risk?'

'I knew you were cross, darling. But – '

'How could you possibly have known I was cross? I thought I kept it hidden.'

Anne and Gerald burst into laughter.

'Oh, sweetheart, you wouldn't be able to keep it hidden if you tried. When you're cross you turn your head to one side and you press your lips together and the sides of your mouth turn down – '

'And you blow through your nose,' added Gerald.

'What a very attractive picture the two of you paint of me. A sort of disgruntled walrus. Presumably you also think – '

'Do you remember, Dad,' said Gerald, 'that time when I was still at secondary school, and I came home and said I had something to tell you, but I would only say it if you promised not to get all steamed up and cross before I had a chance to finish?'

I sighed. It could have been any one of a number of occasions when I had forgotten the convoluted nature of my son's sense of humour and taken the bait like some half-witted fish that hadn't eaten for a month.

'Go on, then. Remind me.'

'Well, I said I'd got something to tell you about one of my teachers, but, like I said, I made you promise that you wouldn't get cross whatever I said or I wasn't going to say another word.'

'And?'

'You promised, like a good little parent. So then I told you that one of my teachers was taking drugs. You wasted no time at all before going straight into the old compressed lips, mouth turned down, blowing through the nose, disgruntled walrus routine. Then I said that it didn't really matter because students in the classes of teachers who took drugs were statistically likely to live longer than students whose teachers didn't take drugs. Then you looked at me as if I'd gone raving mad and asked me what the hell I was drivelling on about – I think those were your exact words. And I said – '

'I remember what you said,' laughed Anne, 'because I was on the verge of throttling you as well, I seem to recall. You said that the students of those on drugs live longer because when a teacher takes drugs – his pupils dilate.'

'It seems wrong to me,' I said, shaking my head sadly, 'to exhume a joke that always was too thin to live, just when it was settling quietly down to decompose and be forgotten forever. Anyway, we've gone off the point. I was asking you, Anne, what made you take the big risk of mentioning the tour to Angels before we'd even seen her dance?'

'Well,' said Anne hesitantly, 'at the risk of sounding rather silly again, I think it was because there are times – not that often, but just now and then – when you have to draw a shape in the air so that God can fill it in and colour it and turn it into a real picture. I really believe that. But you're right, it was a risk, and if I'd turned out to be wrong you would have had every reason to get very walrus-ish indeed.'

'I wonder,' I said, 'if we might forget the walrus image.'

'That shouldn't be a problem, Dad,' said Gerald, grinning at me as he has done since he was a very small boy, 'as long as you never ever get cross again.'

Rang Barry after tea just to check that inviting another person is okay, and when Angels and Leonard came round this evening Anne and I repeated how much we'd enjoyed her dancing, and asked how she would feel about coming with us on the tour and contributing two or three dances each evening. Rarely seen pleasure and fear and excitement chase each other in circles as they did on Angels' face when we said that. Thynn was almost incoherent with joy at the thought of his new girlfriend coming along with the rest of us, but, unsurprisingly, he almost immediately flew off into one of his crescendo panics.

'This is amazing!' he said. 'I really never thought we'd be together on the tour! Wait! Hold on a minute, what about the hotels and all that? They've all been booked. There won't be any spare rooms. We can't sleep in the same room because I'm a Christian, worse luck! She can't come after all. Wait a minute! She can have my room and I won't come. No, that's no good because then we wouldn't be together on the tour and I was only offering to give up my room so that she could go on the tour so that we could be together on the tour, and if I don't come there won't have been any point in giving up my room because we won't be – '

'Leonard, dear,' interrupted Anne, knowing that this sort of thing can go on for ever or until Leonard bursts or faints from exhaustion, 'I'm sure there'll be no trouble at all with booking extra rooms, and if there is we can always sort something out. Gerald could have a camp-bed in our room if necessary, or something like that. Couldn't you, Gerald?'

'Yes, of course,' said Gerald, smiling, 'and you usually get a bit of a reduction for a child sharing, don't you? Dad'll have to promise to read me to sleep, though, just like the old days.'

'Adrian,' Angels forehead was creased with worry, 'I honestly would love to come. I'm sure I shall be terribly, terribly nervous, but it would be wonderful to be with Leonard and the rest of you and do some real dancing.' She flushed. 'I mean – of course I don't mean that it's not real dancing up at Clay House. It's just – well, you know what I mean. The only thing that really troubles me is that – well, you're all Christians, and the evenings will be all about Christian things and the fact is that I'm not one.'

She gazed questioningly at Anne and I with her big, soft brown eyes.

'Are you sure you want someone like me involved? It won't – it won't spoil it in some way?'

Sometimes Anne and I seem to know the same thing at exactly the same time. Not often. Just sometimes. This was one of those times.

I said, 'Angels, I'm quite sure that God wants you to come with us, whether you believe in him or not.'

'You dance like an angel,' said Anne, 'and God has always used angels to bring messages to people. You're just what he needs and exactly what we need. I'm so glad you're coming.'

Anne spent the rest of the evening phoning around, and by the time we were both in bed tonight the accommodation was sorted.

'And,' added Anne, as she turned her bedside light off, 'that's without you having to read bedtime stories to little Gerald.'

Why did I feel a passing pang of sadness when she said that?

WEDNESDAY, 19 SEPTEMBER

Promised Leonard that I would meet him in the church hall this evening to practise setting-up and operating the back-projector and its screen. He collected it from a place in town called 'Sights and Sounds' earlier today, and tonight was our only chance to get the equipment out and have a look at it before the tour starts on Friday.

Arrived to find Thynn standing in the corner of the hall clutching the sides of his head with his hands and staring fixedly at a big, square metal frame lying in the middle of the floor, with a huge sheet of off-white canvas-like material attached to it at a couple of points.

Approached Leonard rather tentatively and asked him what was going on.

'I did make the long straight metal thing into a square,' he said in a small, barely contained, traumatised voice, his eyes still fixed on the middle of the room. 'It didn't want to go into a square, you know. It bit me and it pinched me and it tried to go straight again, but I fought it and shouted at it and rolled around on the floor with it, and in the end it gave in. It's a square now. Look!' He laughed a little mad laugh and pointed with a wavering arm. 'It's a square. I did that! It was me who turned the long straight metal thing into a square.'

'Well, go-o-o-od!' I said, as gently and encouragingly as I could. 'Well done, Leonard. You're right, it is a great big square, just like it's supposed to be, and all we have to do now is fix the screen cloth by pressing it onto all those metal studs around the edge of the frame.'

'Oh, but I've tried,' said Thynn, turning his gaze towards me and rolling his eyes round in his head like a character from one of those old melodramas who's been to hell and back and will bear the marks for ever. 'I've tried, Adrian, but the evil cloth thing – well, it's out to get me. It wants to drive me mad and kill me in the end.'

He swivelled his head and looked up at the clock over the serving hatch.

'I came early, you know, to see if I could have it all done by the time you came. It took me half an hour to turn the long metal thing into a square, and since then I've been trying to put the cloth on.'

He advanced a wary step or two towards the centre of the hall.

'It looked so easy, you see. I began by fastening a corner – that was no problem, and then I just went along one side pressing the studs in as I went. I did a whole side. I enjoyed it. I was so happy. And then I did another side. I thought it was all going to be all right. But when I started to do the third side I couldn't

48

do it. It wouldn't stretch far enough and when I got down flat on the floor and really pulled it, the whole of the side I'd done first came out, and when I'd finished fixing the third side right along to the end, the first side wouldn't stretch far enough, and when I went and really pulled that one the second side came out. And then I started jumping up and down on the cloth and screaming at it and a lady came in to clean the hall and ran out again.'

'Gosh! So what did you do then?'

'Well, then I decided I was going to calm right down and try again. I crept up on that cloth like a lion stalking a zebra, Adrian, and I just pressed one stud in and walked casually off out of the door as if I was going home. Then I strolled back unexpectedly and did another one. Then another, and then another until I'd got two whole sides done again. Then I did a sudden fierce rush at the third side, threw myself on it with a roar and pulled the cloth as hard as I could to get the thingy over the stud.'

'And?'

Leonard turned and, clutching my lapels, spoke feverishly into my face.

'They *all* came out. *All* of them, Adrian. They all flew out and the cloth thing made a sort of flappy laughing sound and leapt into the air and wrapped itself round my head and tried to whip me to death and suffocate me, but I somehow managed to escape and I've been here in this corner ever since, waiting for you to come so that we can strangle it together if it starts any more trouble.'

'Leonard,' I said, gently detaching him from my jacket, 'this cloth screen is an inanimate object. It has no brain. It's just a

50

matter of using the right technique to get the cloth fixed on. It's bound to be tricky because it has to be stretched very tight, you see. The slides won't show up properly if it isn't.'

Thynn shook his head slowly and cynically, looking at me like a man who, having been chased by some wild, supposedly extinct creature, is having trouble making the people back in civilisation believe what happened to him.

'Well, you can do it,' he said, 'I'm not going near it again. It hates me.'

Leaving Thynn looking on from a distance, I approached the monster in the middle of the hall and studied it for a moment or two. As it happened, I did know the secret of fixing the screen to the frame, because I'd done it once before for a church event. In fact, it was childishly simple once you knew how. For a moment or two I enjoyed the mental image of me quickly and efficiently succeeding where Leonard had failed. Ironic really, the whole thing, when you considered my chronic lack of practical skills.

Let Leonard do it.

Funny, isn't it, how little things come into your mind sometimes. Little things that could be from God or might be a load of nonsense, like the famous time when I thought God might have told me to buy a tree-frog and call it Kaiser Bill. I thought I was never going to hear the last of that. In fact, come to think of it, I never have heard the last of it. They still bring it up when they think I'm getting too big for my boots.

Let Leonard do it.

'Tell you what, Leonard, why don't you try fixing the studs to two of the diagonally opposite corners, and then work your way along from there?'

'You think that might work?'

'I think it's worth a try.'

Like a hunter approaching a wounded buffalo, he edged nervously up to the screen and, with one eye clenched tight shut, detached the two studs that had remained fixed after his last foray. A few minutes later, with disconcerting ease, as far as Leonard was concerned, the screen was fixed tightly across the frame, every stud firmly in place.

'Well,' said Thynn, standing back and surveying the scene of his triumph, 'that's got that done! I think I'd better be in charge of this side of things during the tour, Adrian. There's a bit of a knack to it. Best if you leave it to me. After all,' he added playfully, 'we wouldn't want anything to get broken, would we?'

Toyed with the idea of smashing one of the hall chairs over his head, but decided to keep the blessing to myself ...

THURSDAY, 20 SEPTEMBER

Tour starts tomorrow!

Everyone round this evening for coffee, last-minute plans and a chance for Barry to meet the others. Edwin, our elder was here as well, representing my support group from the church.

Felt a bit worried before our benefactor arrived, and even worse after he'd been here for a while. Began to seriously wonder if it wouldn't be better to go back to doing the whole thing on a shoestring. I think the fact that he's putting up the money must have gone to his head a little bit. A great chunk of the early part of the evening was taken up with Ingstone lecturing us at length on how we should 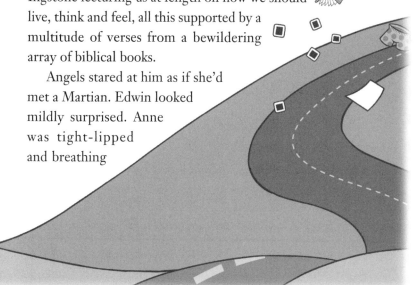 live, think and feel, all this supported by a multitude of verses from a bewildering array of biblical books.

Angels stared at him as if she'd met a Martian. Edwin looked mildly surprised. Anne was tight-lipped and breathing through her nose. Leonard became so boggle-eyed that he could easily have been a Martian. Gerald stayed quiet for a long time. In fact, he said next to nothing right up to the point when Ingstone, possibly realising at last that he had totally monopolised the conversation, stopped lecturing us on the Bible for long enough to ask Gerald what sort of things were happening in his parish.

Couldn't help feeling apprehensive when Gerald started speaking in the very serious voice that, as Anne and I know only too well, usually means that he is planning to talk absolute nonsense.

'Ah, well, Barry, our parish includes one of the big London commons,' he said, 'so we do quite a bit of work with people who are – well, you know.'

'People who are . . . ?'

Gerald puffed his cheeks out, cupped one hand several inches in front of his face, then clenched the other hand and pushed it out as far in front of him as it would go before drawing it back again.

'You know . . .'

Barry's eyes were like dinner-plates.

'Oh – you mean people who are . . .'

'Exactly.'

'Ah, those people.'

'Yes, that's right, people whose lives are not really fulfilled without regular opportunities for the casual use of wind instruments.'

'Without – '

'I don't know if you know this, Barry, but research shows that at least one in every twenty-five men and an unknown percentage of women actually owns a wind instrument of some kind. Think of that. Most keep them hidden away, of course. Times haven't changed that much. There's still a lot of intolerance about. Sometimes whole families are amazed to discover that the father, brother, son or grandfather they thought they knew so well has had a French horn or a bugle or perhaps even a tuba tucked away in his closet for years.'

'A bugle – '

'And down on the heath near us is where people like that go to find folk with the same – well, the same needs and problems.'

'They do?!'

'Oh, yeah, if you go down there after dark, late on a summer's night, as you walk along you'll hear rustlings from the undergrowth and bushes. You'll catch sight of indistinct figures flitting from shadow to shadow, each one clutching a wind instrument of some kind and hoping to find someone with the same proclivities who's up for a quick duet in a dark corner with no strings attached – well, there wouldn't be with wind instruments, would there? The way it works is, a man with, say, a tenor bassoon happens on someone else with a tuba behind a tree. Just a few whispered words of greeting and the quick selection of a key, and before you know it they're into "Colonel Bogie". A few minutes later it's all over. Both of them slip away into the darkness, and that's probably the last they'll ever see of each other. Sadly, Barry, it's just the short-term harmony they're craving for, you see, not any kind of long-term musical involvement. If you walk down there at midnight some nights you can hear little bursts of music all over the common. But aren't we lucky to know the right Christian response to people like that, Barry?'

Barry seemed to be hypnotised by the deadly seriousness of Gerald's manner.

'Are we? I mean – yes, yes, of course we are. I mean – what do you mean?'

'Oh, you know, Barry, as well as I do. We hate the trombone, but we love the trombone-player, don't we?'

'Love the trombone-player . . . ,' repeated Ingstone dazedly.

'Personally,' said Gerald, 'I don't find it easy. I have to struggle with a real inner revulsion against these casual musicians. Don't you agree?'

Barry was literally dumbfounded. I've seen Gerald have this effect on people before. He delivers this kind of nonsense with such fluent gravity that an unwary listener can end up in a sort of trance, mentally sorting through what he or she has just heard before so much as risking a reply. That's what happened with Barry tonight. I don't suppose it will subdue him for long, but at least it shut him up for the rest of the evening.

Lots of animated discussion about the tour after that. Angels is obviously very nervous, but excited as well. Leonard still can't get over the fact that he'll be able to be with his beloved for a whole week when he had thought they'd be apart.

Edwin said a prayer for the tour, but only a short one. I think he realised that poor Angels was already rather shell-shocked by Ingstone. Anne whispered to me that she'd take her aside at some point tomorrow and explain that Barry was not the platonic ideal of a Christian man.

Towards the end of the evening Edwin said, with a little smile playing round his lips, 'So, Gerald, apart from your valuable ministry to lonely musicians, what else have you been up to?'

'Oh, just carrying on getting settled into the parish,' said Gerald. 'It's not too bad now, but when I first got there I had to put up with one or two people telling me how wonderful the last man had been, and how they never expected to see his like again. But, these previous-curate-worshippers always indicated, I was very welcome anyway, miserably inferior substitute though I was. I tell you what, the bloke before me seems to have been a cross between Billy Graham and Popeye – with a dash of Cary Grant thrown in, as far as a few of the older ladies in the church were concerned. I began to feel quite intimidated.'

'But you're getting on fine now, aren't you?' said Anne.

'Oh, well, I spent some time in prayer,' replied Gerald, 'and God gave me an inspiration – a way to make a breakthrough with the congregation.'

Barry nodded approvingly. Gerald was speaking his language now.

'And in what form did the answer to your prayer appear?' he enquired.

'Ah,' said Gerald, 'it's really rather interesting, actually. It came in the form of – well, why don't you have a guess? Go on – have a guess.'

'I would imagine,' hazarded Barry, 'that the Lord furnished you with an inspired word from scripture that reached the hearts and minds of those present and persuaded them that a new beginning was dawning on the horizon of their spiritual perceptions.'

'Well, that sounds very impressive,' said Gerald, 'but actually it was doughnuts.'

'Oh, lovely!' exclaimed Angels.

'Yes, I bought a load of jam doughnuts and gave them out with the drinks after the morning service one Sunday. That seemed to do the trick.'

Edwin swung back in his chair, laughing and clapping his hands.

'What a privilege it is for us,' he chuckled, 'to serve a God who answers prayer with doughnuts. Don't you agree, Barry?'

'Er, yes,' said Barry, trouble and doubt creasing his brow, 'yes, I suppose it is.'

'Actually,' said Gerald, 'I only had one doughnut, but I blessed it and broke it and it seemed to go round okay. Cheaper that way, of course.'

'That was a joke, Barry,' said Anne.

'Oh, I see,' replied Barry.

Do hope Barry doesn't get to the end of this week and feel all this money of his has been wasted.

We shall see.

FRIDAY, 21 SEPTEMBER

Away we go!

Equipment and luggage and paintings all stowed carefully away in the back of our big hired vehicle. Lots of room for human beings as well!

Such a joy to have Gerald sharing the driving with me on this tour. He never seems to get tired like I do, and we'll be able to have some good chats when I'm up at the front beside him. Only problem with me sitting up front is that my son is less than respectful about my map-reading skills.

Fifteen minutes after we set off this morning he glanced across to me as I was sorting out travel details and said, 'Ah. So you've got the directions, then, have you, Dad?'

He sounded to me like a busy surgeon who's just received the news that Dracula has been put in charge of the blood-bank.

'Yes,' I replied with dignity, 'I have got the directions

and I have also got the road atlas. Do you have a problem with that? I would humbly submit that I can read a map as well as anyone else in this vehicle.'

'Oh, yes, Dad, no need to be defensive. You do read a map perfectly well, it's just that – well, how can I put it? I've got it. You know those programmes on the television where they have members of the public talking about how they've fallen hopelessly in love with their grandmother's ferret and it's split the family, and the ferret's there and the grandmother's there and they all argue?'

'No, I'm not sure that I do.'

'Oh, come on! You know – those daytime things where someone always says that it's what you are on the inside that counts and not how you look on the outside, and everyone applauds despite the fact that none of them really agrees. And people are always talking about what's going to happen at the end of the day for some reason. Know the sort of thing I mean?'

'I was asked to be in one of those once,' interjected Thynn from the back.

'Were you really, Leonard?' said Angels. 'What was it about?'

'It was a programme called *Killjoy*, or something like that, and they wanted to get together lots of people whose memories were really bad to talk about how they coped on a day-to-day thingamabob.'

'And what was it like being on the programme?'

'I don't know. I forgot to go.'

Gerald chuckled.

'Now, now, Leonard,' he called over his shoulder, 'I think that might be one of your very entertaining little porkies, like the one you once told us about your Irish cousin – Finnegan Thynn, I think you said he was called – who used to smuggle Bibles *out* of China in the sixties.'

'Leonard!' Angels pretended to be deeply shocked. 'Do you really tell porky-pies? That's very naughty!'

Sounds of a play-fight floated over from the back of the van.

'You'll excuse me attempting to navigate the conversation back to the point, Gerald, but – '

'That's very good, Dad,' interrupted Gerald seriously, 'navigating the conversation back to the point – very good.'

'Perhaps you wouldn't mind just telling me what those silly programmes have to do with the way I read maps.'

'Ah, right! Yes, of course. Well, it's just that I seem to remember reading that they always put a sort of one or two minute delay on these so-called live programmes in case anyone does or says something really dreadful.'

'So? What if they do?'

'Well, your map-reading is a bit like that. It's what you might call retrospective navigation.'

'Retrospective navigation? What on earth is that supposed to mean?'

'It means that you always know exactly where we should have turned off a couple of minutes after the time when we should have done it. So ideally you'd begin by giving me the direction after next, except that the whole thing would be completely thrown out by the fact that you haven't given me the very next direction, so nothing would go right after that anyway, would it?'

Felt a bit nettled really.

I said, 'That may all be very funny, Gerald, but the fact is that I have been reading maps for years. I know exactly where we are going and precisely when and where we should turn off.'

'Left here, Gerald!' called Anne suddenly from the back of the van.

'Oh, thanks, Mum! Just in time. Sorry, Dad, what were you saying?'

Despite the silly cackling that followed this nonsense, there is someone who is even worse at map-reading than me. If Leonard hadn't been in the back of the van I would have told Gerald about the first and last time that Thynn was allowed to navigate for me. As far as I can remember he said something along the following lines:

'Right, Adrian, we're on a long red line going through the middle of a pink patch, and there's some little white worms squiggling around quite near us, and we should soon come to a big word in black capital letters written across a round circle just next to a grey splodge. And if we come to a blue wavy line with some numbers running along it we'll know we've gone wrong.'

Remember stopping the car at that point and taking the map away from him forever. We arrived at the grey splodge without any further help from Leonard.

However, all that aside, it's very exciting to be on our way. Here we go! Off on our tour! On the road! Rock and roll! Well, a series of illustrated Christian talks anyway ...

Stopped at Bowlstoke for lunch today. Left the others eating and took the opportunity to pop into my publisher's office to see what's going on. Made my way to the office of Harry Waits-Round, who heads up the Christian book division at Wringem, Dooley and Stitch. Knocked on his door. From the other side a voice sounding heavy with frustration, despair, irritation and hatred for all mankind said, 'Yesss! What now, for goodness' *sake*?'

Opened the door and witnessed a miracle. Harry Waits-Round turned into a poem of joy and optimism before my very eyes.

He said, 'Adrian! Great to see you! What a wonderful surprise! Take a seat and I'll get you some coffee.'

Thought he was going to float up to the ceiling, inflated, apparently, by the sheer joy of seeing my face. Can't honestly say I usually have this effect on people. Perhaps he sees qualities in me that others miss.

'How's the new book going?' I asked when we were settled with coffee and Harry had got his rapture a little more under control.

Often wonder if publishers have to go to a special college to learn the language they speak. I suppose it's a sort of code, but unless you've learned it you can spend quite a long time never quite understanding what the other person is talking about.

'We're *very* encouraged,' said Harry, nodding slowly and earnestly, 'we really are.'

'So that means. . . ?'

'We're proud to be able to include it on our list, and it's sold out very reasonably.'

'Sold out? Great! Do you mean you've sold all the ones that you've printed?'

'No, no, better than that! I mean that it's sold out into the shops very reasonably.'

'Oh, I see. So – I don't quite understand, how can that be better than selling all the books that you've printed?'

'Ah, well, because in my view what we have here is a book with a very long shelf-life.' He gestured dismissively and contemptuously with one hand at a best-seller list on the wall. 'This book is not one of these three-week wonders that sells twenty or thirty thousand and then you never hear of it again.'

'I see.'

Secretly rather fancied the idea of my book being a three-week wonder that sold twenty or thirty thousand and was then never heard of again. Didn't like to say so, though. After all, he's the publisher. He must know what he's talking about.

'So how many has it actually sold to the public – *out* of the shops, I mean?'

'*Out* of the shops?' said Harry, knitting his brows and blinking as though I'd introduced him to some bewilderingly novel concept. 'Out of the *shops*? Ah, I see what you mean. Well, the first thing to say is that we haven't had the returns in yet.'

'The returns?'

'Yes, you see, the bookshops return the books that they don't sell, and – '

'Even the ones with a long shelf-life?'

'Err, yes. Oh! By the way, I seem to remember there's some mail for you in the next pod.'

'Pod?'

'That's what we call the work-spaces. Pods. Come on!'

There were three or four people in the 'pod' next to Harry's. My mail consisted of three letters, one of which was strangely soft and pulpy to the touch.

One of the girls said, 'We've been wondering what's in that one.'

Opened it on the spot in front of everybody. Rather embarrassing. Inside there was a brassiere. Shocked silence. Took the accompanying letter from the envelope and read it out loud.

Dear Adrian Plass,

I enjoy reading your books and I always tell other people how good they are. In one of your books you make the following statement:

'I read somewhere recently that the travelling Christian speaker is likely to face three main temptations. These are, in no particular order, sex, power and money. Well, all I can say is that I must be on the wrong circuit. I'm always on the look-out for opportunities to heroically resist the queue of seductive temptresses that should be waiting outside my hotel door, but so far not one has put in an appearance. I'm not complaining, Lord – honestly!'

I thought that as you are feeling a bit put out at never having the chance to battle with temptation I would send you my bra as a sort of consolation prize. Hope it helps.

Yours Sincerely,
Eileen

Another shocked silence, and then a very Christian looking chap who was sitting at the desk frowned, tilted his head to one side and said, 'Hmm, yeah.'

Difficult to convey the very particular nuance of that 'Hmm, yeah'. In just two sounds it managed to convey the message: 'Look, we Christians are as able and willing to enjoy a jape as the next chap. The fact is, though, that some things are just a little too far beyond the pale for us to seriously regard them as matters for fun, and I very much fear that this, although it may appear to have a lighter side, is one of those things.'

Talk about code!

We all stood dismally staring at the bra hanging from my hand, trying to feel the message of the 'Hmm, yeah', until Harry Waits-Round suddenly exploded into laughter and set all the others off, including the man at the desk. Relief!

Was out of the door and on my way back to meet the others when I realised that I still had no idea how many copies of my book had been sold. I'll ring Harry Waits-Round in a couple of days and really pin him down.

Our first evening event has happened! Began badly, but ended well.

I don't believe there is a truly murderous bone in my body, but if I ever do attack someone physically in a fit of rage it will probably be one of those people who do the 'sound' for their church on a part-time basis. I freely admit that most of them are good, competent, nice people who do their very best, but there is a small minority who are either used by the devil to tempt me to sin, or by God to teach me about forgiveness and restraint. The man who did the sound at St James the Hardly

Visible at All on our first evening must have been one of the former.

There were problems even before that. I left the others to settle in at the hotel while I went early on my own to check out the venue. After banging on a succession of blank, unyielding doors that looked as if they hadn't been opened since 1870, I was finally let in by someone I took to be the caretaker, a square, heavy man with a bald head and long arms, whose expression of indignant incomprehension never altered from that moment (as far as I was concerned anyway) until the moment when we left. He glared at me as if I was a thirteen-year-old vandal clutching a can of spray-paint in my hand. Not encouraged by his first words.

'Wot's all the bangin' for, then?'

I said, 'I'm really sorry, I was just trying to make someone hear me. I'm one of the group that are putting on the presentation tonight. I was told I could come along earlier to have a look round.'

He shook his head with gloomy relish.

'No-one told me *nothing* about anyone coming along earlier, and I'm supposed to be the caretaker.'

'Oh, well, I'm sorry, I assumed the vicar would have mentioned it to you. My name,' I added modestly, 'is Adrian Plass.'

Not impressed.

'My name's Mr Purbeck and it don't matter if you're Mother Theresa. No-one told me *nothing* about no-one coming – '

'Well, anyway, would it be all right if I came in now, just to – you know – see how the land lies?'

'See how the land lies? See how what land lies?'

'Well, you know the sort of thing I mean. Work out where the books are going to go and – '

'No-one told me nothing about no books. Tables for books is all locked away in the big cupboard at the back.'

'Oh, I see. Well, do you have a key to the cupboard, please?'

He fumed for a moment, clearly reluctant to admit that the universe could possibly be anything but a dark, hopeless, keyless place.

'Have I got a *key*? Is *that* what you're asking me?'

'Er, yes, have you got a key to the cupboard where the tables are?'

'Oh, I've *got* a key,' he said, his manner suggesting that his possession of the key was a tiny and really almost irrelevant factor in solving the question of how one might open the cupboard. 'I've got a *key*, but . . .' A sudden inspiration. 'I've got my other work to do. No-one said nothing to me about shifting tables out of the cupboard all afternoon.'

'All right, well, if you would please be kind enough to just open the cupboard for me, I'll get the tables out myself. I won't trouble you at all, I promise. You weren't about to go home or anything, were you?'

A contest between truth and the longing to tell me that he had been about to go home raged across Mr Purbeck's irascible features for a second or two. Truth won by a short head.

'I wasn't about to go home, no – not *home*.'

Mr Purbeck's tone seemed to imply that, whilst he had not actually been about to go home, he *had* been on the very cusp of doing something else so similar to being about to go home as to be virtually indistinguishable.

I said, 'Oh, good, because I wouldn't want to put you to any trouble. I'll just get the tables out and then I'll go and have a quiet look inside the church to get an idea – '

'Hah! Lights are orf in the church.'

'Oh, are they? Well, couldn't I just – you know – switch them on?'

Satisfaction brought a triumphant gleam to the caretaker's eye, while deep offence added a tightening to his jaw. Paradoxically, I got the distinct impression that, in some obscure way, I was easily the best thing that had happened to him for quite a long time. Others might fail him dismally and continually by doing the right thing at the right time and making sure they told him first. I, on the other hand, was generously confirming his innate belief that the entire population of the world woke up each morning filled with a single burning desire, namely, to upset Mr Purbeck by asking for things that he hadn't been told nothing about.

'Switches are locked up in the switchbox. When I've got other work to do I can't go running and skipping and dancing around after folk with my bunch of keys every time they decide they want to open something willy-nilly, specially when no-one's told me nothing about – '

'I really don't want you to go running and skipping and dancing – particularly not skipping and dancing – around after me with your bunch of keys, Mr Purbeck. Only the cupboard where the tables are and the switchbox. If you could just open those two for me, I really would be ever so grateful and I promise you, on my word of honour, I won't ask you to unlock anything else until the time when you were told we were coming.'

'I shall be speaking to the vicar,' said Mr Purbeck ominously.

After opening the cupboard and the box for me he hung around near where I was for a few minutes, fiddling with things, presumably hoping that I might inconvenience him in some further way. I'm afraid I must have been a great disappointment. I asked for nothing else until the others turned up. Hoped he felt able to forgive me.

Looked forward to some sanity when the others arrived. Instead I had to deal with Thynn, who, despite having mastered the assembly of his screen, went shrieking hysterically around the church about the fact that there was nowhere for his back-projector to go that would allow an eight-foot throw between projector and screen. Then, on arriving, Angels turned white with terror when she saw that it really was all going to happen, burst into tears and said that the ambience was all wrong, the ceiling was too high, the floor was too hard and the lights weren't bright enough. Then she launched into a another long speech about directional cross-currents and spiritual alignment and atavistic inhibitions and goodness knows what else. Finally, she said that she couldn't possibly, *possibly* dance in the tiny space that I had allocated to her, and she wanted to know if I was really trying to say that I didn't want her to dance at all, in which case wouldn't it be better for all concerned if she just went home?

Not exactly Acts of the Apostles, is it?

Solved Thynn's problem by taking him off into a corner and quietly threatening to kill him, and by standing the screen on one of those obscure pieces of ecclesiastical furniture (supplied by Mr Purbeck, despite the fact that no-one had told him nothing about no-one needing obscure pieces of ecclesiastical furniture) at the side of the raised area at the front of the church.

Left Leonard to get the thing set up and arrange the slides in the carousel.

Left Angels to Anne, who arrived with Gerald, a bottle of milk, a bag of sugar, a flask of tea and, most important of all, herself.

Just breathing a sigh of relief that calm had descended again, when the sound man arrived. Thin, lank-haired, smartly dressed but slightly dishevelled, he had the air of a man who has not yet had his gin and tonic after arriving home from work after a crowded journey on the train. Shook hands rather briskly and said, 'Verne Fowler. I do sound for the church. Actually it's my system. You tonight's thing? Vicar asked me to come along early and do a sound-check.'

Confessed that I was tonight's thing.

After a plugging in of this and that, and a twiddling of knobs, and a thump of cupboards opening and closing and a clang and clatter of microphone stands being put up and adjusted, Fowler stopped huffing and puffing and sighing heavily and dashing distractedly around and announced that he was ready for me to do a sound-check.

'Right, off you go,' he called from where he stood behind his equipment at the back of the church, 'just speak clearly into the mike and I'll adjust it from here.'

Never have known what to say into microphones when they're being tested. Been a bit wary generally of sound technicians ever since one of them at a festival called out to me, 'Do you want more bottom in your fold back?' and Gerald, who was standing at the side, annoyed him by shouting back, 'They've got special seminars for people like you, mate!'

Decided to be very orthodox on this occasion.

I said, 'One, two! Testing, one, two! One, two! One, two, three!'

Made some clicking, popping, kissing noises as well, like they do. Finally read a bit from a poem I was going to do later.

'Right,' called Fowler, 'that's fine! I'll get off home. See you later.'

I'd nearly let him go before realising that I had detected one small flaw in his sound system.

'Err, Verne, sorry to hold you up, but there is just one little thing.'

Fowler, who was halfway to the door and presumably pursuing his phantom gin and tonic as though it was the Holy Grail, lifted one hand and exasperatedly swept his hair to the back of his head.

'*What*? It sounds fine.'

'Right. But er it doesn't seem to be actually amplifying my voice.'

'What do you mean?'

'What do I mean? Well, my voice isn't being made any louder. I mean, surely the whole point of the sound-system is to make it easier for people to – '

He put his hands on his hips and scowled at me as he interrupted.

'It's on exactly the same setting as the vicar uses in church every Sunday morning,' he said crossly, 'and it sounds perfectly all right to me.'

Knew that if I didn't persist now the whole evening would consist of me shouting at people who had done nothing to deserve it.

'I still think that we ought to – '

'Have you done any speaking before? Because if you have you'll know that the important thing is what the audience hear, not how loud you think your voice ought to sound in your own ears. The sound is fine. Now, if that's all I really must be going.'

Fought to overcome my disease of politeness. Afraid I succeeded.

I said, 'I hear what you say, Mr Fowler, but that's because you're shouting. I don't see how the people who are coming tonight will be able to hear what I say unless I bawl like a barrow-boy. When we did the test I was speaking in my normal voice and it never got any louder. Forgive me if I'm wrong, but I always assumed that a sound system, however excellent in every other respect, falls a tad short of the ideal when it provides no amplification whatsoever. Or am I being naive? Are my expectations way too high.'

Saying something under his breath that sounded like 'Bloody amateurs!', Fowler stalked back to his desk and said through gritted teeth, 'Go on, then. Talk!'

Started to read again, but stopped when I noticed that Fowler seemed to have been taken ill. A deep flush had suffused his face and moments later he dropped abruptly from sight behind the sound desk. About to rush over to help when he resurfaced, still crimson, and said, in a completely different tone, 'Okay, give it a try now.'

Oh, the sweet, sweet sound of rich, effortless, proper amplification! So reassuring! Such a comfort! Fowler approached me, contrition written all over his face. Extended a weary arm to shake my hand.

'Sorry, mate,' he said, 'forgot to switch it on. Far too busy trying to do it without really doing it so I could get home quickly. Ended up making a complete fool of myself. No hard feelings?'

'Hard feelings?' I replied, 'you've got to be joking! Other people making mistakes is what keeps me going. No, I'm just glad that it works. Thanks.'

As he walked off, couldn't help remembering one rain swept night at home when Anne and I were woken at three o'clock in the morning by a terrible noise in the street outside. Pulled the curtain to one side and saw that the noise came from a car alarm four or five houses up the street. Must have been set off by the heavy rain. We watched as the lady who owned the car came flying, wild-haired, out of her house in a dressing-gown and spent several frantic, rain-soaked minutes getting the thing to switch itself off. Next day she did a little tour of the local houses, apologising for the disturbance her car alarm must have caused. No idea what other people said, but my response was very clear.

'Oh, no,' I said, 'please, please don't apologise. The noise did wake me, and at first I thought it must be something to do with me, because – well, things often are to do with me. Then I looked through the curtains and saw you come out to sort your car out, and all I could think was, "Oh, thank you, God! That's not me over there! It's not my car alarm that's been set off by the rain. I'm here in my warm, dry room and it's not my fault. In fact I want to thank you. I enjoyed every *minute* of it!"'

Interested to hear how Gerald would get on with Mr Purbeck, the caretaker. Listened to them while I was helping Thynn to sort his stuff out. Gerald had obviously got the measure of the man. Dialogue went roughly as follows.

GERALD: We could really do with some steps on the side here, Mr Purbeck, so that the dancer doesn't have to exit from the front. Any chance of you having a little double step or something tucked away anywhere?

PURBECK: *(happily and predictably)* No-one told me nothing about no steps being needed.

GERALD: *(completely unabashed and in exactly the same aggressive tone as Mr Purbeck)* What! Well, no-one told me nothing about no-one telling you nothing about no steps being needed. Did anyone tell you about no-one telling me nothing about no-one telling you nothing about no steps being needed? Because if they did, no-one told me nothing about telling you about no-one telling me nothing about no-one telling you nothing about no steps being needed, *that's* for sure.

PURBECK: *(rather faintly, after opening and shutting his mouth like a goldfish for a few moments)* Er, well, as it happens I do have a little pair of steps out in the store. I'll – I'll gettem, shall I?

GERALD: That would be great, yes. Oh, and by the way, Mr Purbeck, as I'm sure you've been told, we'll also be needing a thirty foot oak beam carved in the shape of the profile of Georg Brandes, the nineteenth-century Danish literary critic, a giant plastic model of a whale, a concrete mixer filled with shards of opalescent pink Carder glass, a full-size facsimile of the Bayeux tapestry and twelve purple tutu's with reflecting glass beads set at intervals of six inches around the hem. Oh, and I nearly forgot one other little thing, we'll need to knock down the whole of the south wall of the church to give ourselves a bit more space this evening. You okay with all that?

From that moment onwards Mr Purbeck went about his business with a peculiar, tilted little smile on his lips. Somewhere in the depths of his soured soul there must have been a residual memory of something called 'humour'. By going right over the top instead of being heavily polite like me, Gerald seemed to have managed to excavate this thin vein of something that didn't involve constant moaning. The caretaker was clearly puzzled and bemused by the experience, but one thing was for sure, from that moment he was ready and willing to do anything and everything that my son wanted.

Considering it was our first evening, and bearing in mind all the trauma with Leonard and Angels beforehand, the evening was a great success. Angels danced like – well, like an angel, once she had an audience in front of her, and Leonard managed the projector reasonably well, except that some of the slides seemed to be in the wrong order. Must sort that out for next time. Nobody in the audience gave any sign that they'd noticed anyway, so perhaps it didn't matter too much. Lots of interest in Zak's pictures, which we'd set up on some folding screens produced willingly by Mr Purbeck at my son's request. Didn't actually sell any tonight, but people seemed to love them. Gerald's speaking bits were *very* well received, not that I'm envious – well, I am a bit, actually, but then he's my son, so I'm quite proud as well. Looking forward to hearing him speak properly tomorrow evening.

Asked Barry what he'd thought of the evening.

He said, 'Yes, I found it entertaining, but a little light in content.'

Told Anne later how depressing I'd found Barry's comment.

'Don't worry, darling,' she said, 'Barry's glasses need a spot of cleaning. In any case, just think about the fact that we've got Leonard and Angels with us. I know they're hard work, but maybe that's the hard work God wants us to do. Who knows, maybe this whole tour is more for them than for anyone else.'

Hmmm ...

Really wished we'd eaten earlier by the time the meeting ended tonight. We set off in the van to embark on one of those negative patterns that seem to get repeated over and over again, even though we all know they're a very, very *bad* idea indeed. This particular pattern is called: 'Looking for a restaurant and being so picky and critical that by the time you've got exhausted and decided the very first one you found and rejected is better than all the other ones you've seen, that first one, which now shines in your hungry mind like the Holy Grail, has shut, and so have all the others apart from the one that everyone has already agreed is the very last place on earth that you would choose to eat, given the choice.'

Entered 'The Furry Sausage' and collapsed wearily at a table near the window. Looked around. No other customers in the place. The only visible representative of management was slumped in a chair beside the till, her tongue protruding pinkly from between her teeth as she laboriously filled in one of those word-search games that help to bridge that long, tedious gap between birth and death which so challenges the inventiveness and ingenuity of lots of young people nowadays.

As Gerald put it later, the arrival of people who actually wanted to eat registered only the slightest tremor of what looked like irritation on the Richter scale of her attention, but

in the end she sighed heavily, slapped her magazine down on the counter, and hoisted herself laboriously to her feet.

Studied this young lady with fascination as she tottered towards our table, yanking a bent and compressed pad of order forms with difficulty out of a tight back pocket as she approached. Her closest friends and admirers couldn't have seriously claimed that she was dressed to impress. Her tee-shirt, once plain white but now advertising a selection of items from the menu, ended just above her midriff. The waistband of her threadbare black jeans gripped her lower hips like a tourniquet, causing the midriff to protrude and bulge like a small, half-inflated balloon. Leaning her head to one side so that a greasy length of hair fell away from her eyes, she poised a pencil above her pad and regarded us dispassionately.

'Yesss.'

Gathered from her tone that our very existence was annoying and tedious beyond words. The last thing she wanted was *customers* breaking into her latest word-search puzzle. Placed our order as cheerfully as we could, remembering that she was loved by God. Hoped to create a sort of spiritual echo in her. No use. Definitely no material for the testimony paperback on this occasion. She gave a reluctant grunt of acknowledgement, then turned and staggered away in the direction of the kitchen on block-heeled shoes that seemed (with total justification, Gerald suggested) to be trying to throw her onto her face at each step. The gap in her clothing had not been nice from the front. Viewed from behind it had the effect of lowering our spirits to zero.

Gerald shook his head slowly and said, 'That is a more profoundly effective appetite suppressant than anything you could ever get on prescription.'

About three days later, when our meals still hadn't arrived, Angels called out, 'Excuse me, dear, is there any sign of the food yet?'

Our waitress, who was back in her original position, lifted her eyes from her puzzle-book for one despairingly exasperated moment, glanced through a hatch in the direction of the kitchen and said, in a flat, totally uninterested voice, 'It's jus' bein' plated up.'

When our food arrived we realised that we needn't have bothered ordering different dishes. It all tasted exactly the same. Picked listlessly at what had been 'plated up', then crept out as quickly as possible, leaving a large tip because we are hopelessly English.

Can't help contrasting our experience at 'The Furry Sausage' with a meal we had in Los Angeles once, when Anne, Gerald, Thynn and I had a stopover in America on the way back from Australia. The waitress that night was a tall, broadshouldered, powerful-looking blonde called Mabilene. This woman was dressed to kill, had a smile like a flashlight and appeared to fall helplessly in love with each and every one of us at first sight. Greeting us, she expressed her passionate, desperate need to know what sort of a day we had experienced up to this point. We all mumbled that we had had a good day, thanks very much. She received this reassuring news with almost tearful relief and joy, pledging from the depths of her soul that our experience over the next two hours would not only match but exceed the happiness that we had known since waking that morning. Bit more appreciative mumbling and twittering from us, and then it was time for her to take our order.

Something very odd about having your commonplace old comments or choices greeted with admiration and wonder. Mabilene seemed to feel, for instance, that my humble selection of a steak with mushroom sauce scaled hitherto unconquered peaks of creativity, enterprise and sheer brilliance. She was a willing Boswell to my Johnson. She wrote it all down. There was awe and ecstasy in every movement of her pen as she took the order. Mabilene admired my choices *so* much.

I wanted French fries as well.

'Hey!'

And salad.

'Wow!'

And it wasn't just me. No, that night each and every one of us was brilliantly inspired in our choice of dishes. Thynn's request for a dab of French mustard on the side of his plate was nothing short of a masterpiece. We were superb! There really was no other word for it.

When we stood to go at the end of the meal it was as hard for our waitress as if she were having to deal with multiple deaths among the closest members of her family. Mabilene had loved each one of us with her whole dynamic being, but now tragedy had struck. We were leaving and she must lose us. It was the way of the world. For her sake we must promise to guard and protect ourselves for the rest of our lives, and, if Providence should be generous enough to allow that we return to her restaurant at some later date – oh, what an unspeakably sweet, sweet moment that would be for this woman whose previous life had been little more than a rehearsal for this, her encounter with us.

'Have a wonderful night! Have a wonderful life!'

We mumbled again and departed, leaving a moderate tip.

Excruciating moment tonight. Anne and I were relaxing in our room before going to bed, when Anne said, 'Oh, darling, have you got any of those lovely sweets left that we had in the van earlier.'

I said, 'Yes, they're in my coat pocket, the zipped one on the side.'

As Anne got to her feet and started to move towards the coat hanging by the door I suddenly remembered that there was a *bra* in my pocket! With all the business of being late I'd never got round to telling the others what happened at the publishers. Realised, as Anne put her hand out to open the zip on my coat, that there was nothing in the entire universe of language that I could say at this late stage that would be in any way convincing.

I said, in a strangled voice, 'Oh, by the way, Anne, you're really going to laugh! There's – there's a bra in my pocket. Ha-ha! You wouldn't believe – '

'No, said Anne coldly, I don't suppose I would. What do you mean there's a bra in your pocket? Whose bra? Why? Where did you go at lunchtime?'

A nasty moment. All okay in the end. I'd put the woman's letter in my pocket as well, thank goodness.

'In any case,' Anne said, 'as I've told you before, if you did ever have an affair I'd have to organise it, otherwise it would be a complete disaster.'

Agreed in order to keep the peace.

Anne and I composed a joint letter to the lady who'd sent her bra. When Gerald came in to steal my bedtime book he read the letter and almost immediately fell about laughing. When we asked him why, he told us to look at the first line. This is how the letter began:

Dear Eileen,
    First of all, thank you for your support ...

Reminded Anne after we got into bed about our American meal. Asked her if she thought there was a point somewhere between the midriff and Mabilene where restaurant service might be just right.

She said, 'Yes, remember that hotel we stayed at up on the cliffs at Bournemouth, the old-fashioned place that felt as if an Agatha Christie murder could happen there at any moment? It was just right. They cared, but they weren't silly about it. Grace and charm and good food and a bit of tinkly music, that's what it takes, Adrian.'

Asked her if she thought the Last Supper would have been a good meal.

She yawned and said, 'Of course! Grace, charm, good friends, a loaf of bread and a flagon of wine. No tinkly music, but lots of joy, lots of sadness. A *very* good meal.' She smiled sleepily. 'Not quite as good as the next one, though, I don't suppose, the one by the lake. That must have been quite something. Night-night, darling, sleep well.'

SATURDAY, 22 SEPTEMBER

Rather unnerving experience today.

Slept poorly last night. Round about seven this morning I popped out in the van to get a paper and one or two other things, and was nearly hit by a car pulling out from the front of the shop as I pulled in. Had to brake quite sharply.

The other car stopped and the driver, a youngish man with one of those open, friendly faces, stuck his head out of the window and said, 'Really sorry, mate! My fault. I'm afraid I was miles away.'

I'm not at my best in the morning, especially when I haven't slept.

I said, 'It's a shame you weren't miles away. 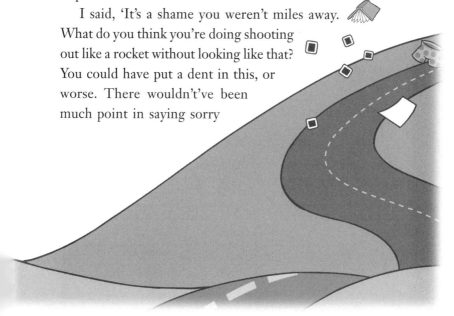 What do you think you're doing shooting out like a rocket without looking like that? You could have put a dent in this, or worse. There wouldn't've been much point in saying sorry then, would there? You want to wake up and think what you're doing.'

The other man looked terribly crestfallen.

'Well, I honestly am sorry,' he said, 'I don't know what else to say.'

'Don't say anything else, then.'

I was beginning to quite relish the situation. I don't get to tell many people off.

'Just be more careful in future. Got it?'

Felt rather pleased with myself in a way. Usually it's me that apologises when someone bumps into me, never mind when I bump into them. I'd given that bloke a piece of my mind he wouldn't forget in a hurry. Made me feel taller, older, more grown-up somehow.

Over breakfast at the hotel this morning Gerald said, 'Barry, you find your way round the Bible really well, don't you? I mean, you're a bit of an expert, aren't you?'

Barry postponed his marmalade spreading operations for a moment and looked warily at Gerald.

'Well, er, yes, I suppose it would be true to say that I have studied the scriptures for many years to a considerable depth, and not, I hope, without profit to myself and others.'

'Exactly,' said Gerald, 'and bearing that in mind, I've got a question for you.'

Barry's eyes gleamed. He laid his knife down.

'I see, and what is your question?'

'Well, first of all, you would agree with me, wouldn't you, that Jesus was without sin? That is right, isn't it? He never sinned, did he?'

Barry said, 'Yes indeed, that is absolutely correct. Hebrews, chapter four, verse fifteen tells us that we have a High Priest who was tempted in every way that we are, but did not sin. Therefore we must approach the – '

'Gosh, you *do* know your Bible, don't you?' interrupted Gerald admiringly. 'So, bearing in mind what we've been saying, we would have to conclude that Jesus never told a lie. Is that correct as well?'

'Yes, of course. In the thirty-second verse of the eighth chapter of the gospel of John, the Lord tells us that we will know the truth and that – '

'He always told the truth?'

'Yes.'

'Okay, well here's my question. Which is the gospel verse in which Jesus quite clearly and openly makes a statement that he knows to be untrue?'

Barry shook his head firmly.

'I cannot believe that there is such a verse,' he replied.

'Oh, yes, there is,' said Gerald, filling his mouth with bacon and fried bread before continuing indistinctly, 'and I bet you can't work out where it is. Bit of a challenge for you there, Barry.'

A few minutes later Gerald finished his breakfast and went back upstairs, still refusing to say which verse he was talking about. Left Barry staring worriedly at his cold toast, presumably running through his mental concordance searching for a clue.

Something tells me we're going to hear more about this . . .

Just got back to the hotel after my lunchtime talk for men. That feeling of being older and more grown-up after blasting the man in the car lasted right up to the moment when I stood up in front of my audience from the local churches and recognised the fellow who'd nearly run into me, sitting on the second row. My heart sank like a stone, right down into my boots. Every word that I'd said outside that shop a few hours ago replayed itself inside my head so loudly and clearly that it seemed as if everyone in the room must be able to hear it. And those were far from being the only words that strung themselves on ribbons in front of my inner eye. I was about to start bleating out all the *stuff* that I always said about the love of God and how it affects the way we deal with other people. All that *stuff*. And there in the second row, staring at me now with a puzzled frown on his face as he tried to work out where he'd met me before, was a man who would know that it was just a load of rubbish.

Then there was my voice. What a contrast there would be between the slightly deeper-than-usual voice that I automatically adopted on occasions like this, and the arch, bullying tones with which I'd earlier dismissed a man who had made an honest mistake and then apologised for it.

I wanted to die, especially as it had now become clear from the expression on the face of the man in the second row that he had recalled the circumstances of our meeting at last. He was staring intently at me, not with anger or distaste, but, what was even worse, with a mixture of disappointment and bewilderment. Two choices, said a voice in my head, plough through uselessly and slide away at the end, or . . .

I'm not like Barry. Verses from the Bible don't often march into my mind and refuse to go away until they've been acted on, but that's exactly what happened this time. I looked it up afterwards and found that it was the second part of verse thirty-two in the eighth chapter of John's gospel.

The truth will set you free.

They were all waiting for me to start. The man in the second row was leaning back now, looking more anxious than anything else. I shall never forget the smile that lit up his face as I began to speak.

'I do have a talk more or less organised,' I said, 'but I hope you'll excuse me if my opening remarks are addressed to the man in the blue jumper, sitting just there, on the second row . . .'

Just after we got moving this afternoon Barry said to Gerald, 'Er, by the way, Gerald, I presume that when you made that reference yesterday to the Lord making an untrue statement, you were simply referring to the fact that he used parables in order to teach, and that the content of those parables was, quite legitimately of course, fiction as opposed to fact. In the fifteenth chapter of Luke, for instance, we learn that – '

'Wrong!' said Gerald. 'Completely wrong! Nothing to do with the parables. Think again, Barry.'

Tonight was the night when we'd arranged for Gerald to do most of the first half on his own. Anne and I excited and nervous about hearing Gerald speak properly for the first time. Almost wished I didn't love him so much. Full of hope and fear. Hope that he would speak really well, and fear that, although he usually has plenty to say, he might turn out to be a useless communicator. Enjoyed the first bit.

He said, 'A lot of you will know that my dad writes and talks a lot about all the people he meets who think they're not good enough for God. The need to reassure and encourage people like that so that they can cheer up and get on with being useful is one of the greatest lessons I've learned, and I want to thank him for that. Today is the first time mum and dad have heard me speak to a congregation or an audience – I haven't let them before – so, following my dad's lead, I'm going to take some things that keep getting turned upside down and try to put them the right way up.'

Passed Anne a tissue and tried to look invisible.

Quite unprepared for the fact that, once Gerald got going, I completely forgot who was speaking. He talked about the priority of knowing and loving Jesus, and how lots of people get distracted by religious 'magic' and waves of this or that and huge projects and dramatic ministries to the point where they forget why they started in the first place. Then he quoted that bit from the seventh chapter of Matthew, where Jesus says: 'Many will say to me on that day, "Lord, Lord, did we not prophesy in your name, and in your name drive out demons and perform many miracles?" Then I will tell them plainly, "I never knew you . . ."'

There wasn't even a suggestion of a sound or a movement in the church as Gerald finished the quotation and, after a pause, went on speaking.

'The thing is,' he said, 'however this passage makes us feel – and in a way it could be quite scary – we have to look at it honestly and bravely and think about what it means. Exactly who gets saved and who doesn't is no business of yours or mine, but it does look as if all sorts of people are going to be surprised, disappointed, perhaps even horrified, when they actually encounter Jesus. Let's imagine some of them.

'"What about me," says one bloke, "you must have known me. I've been a churchgoer all my life. My home was organised. My children were well-behaved and polite. We had regular family Bible-reading sessions. I was on three church committees. I prayed in meetings. I *led* meetings! I went on church weekends. I really got it together. I was part of it – I *am* part of it. I *belong!*"

'"I'm sorry," says Jesus, "I'm sure all of those things were true, but I never knew you."

'"Well, you do know me!" This time it's a very confident, smartly dressed guy. "I addressed huge rallies – thousands of people weeping and praising God and singing. There were wonderful choirs. A bit of a speciality in my meetings. And after I'd spoken and gave the call to the front folk just flooded up to respond to the word they'd heard. Do you know, lots of them fell over flat on their backs when I touched them or just pointed my finger at them. Why, sometimes it was enough just to blow in their direction, and down they went! My ministry was famous! My television shows were famous! The way I looked was famous! Even my *hair* was famous! I was – I was – I was *so* famous!"

'"I have no doubt that you were very, very famous," agrees Jesus, "but I'm afraid I never knew you."

'"Hi, it's me!" calls the next in the queue. "I was a leading figure in healing and deliverance, and I mean a *leading* figure. I wouldn't be able to count how many sufferers received miraculous healing at my hands, and hundreds of people were mightily delivered in the name of Jesus. I devised programmes and systems that got used all over the world. I lectured and I trained and I educated. I – I wrote books and made tapes! I was a household name."

'Jesus slowly shakes his head. "Not in this household, you weren't. I read the books and I heard the tapes. They were very good. I never knew you."

'"I was *the* expert on prayer!" cries another, suddenly filled with panic.

'"Well, I hope you gained a great deal of satisfaction from being known as *the* expert on prayer, because I never knew you."

'"Now look," says a very relaxed, reasonable-looking sort of chap, "I think you'll have to agree that I avoided most of the pitfalls that these others fell into. I didn't get carried away by all the frothy, super-spiritual stuff, nor did I just sit around and do nothing. I read papers, had views, wrote letters, I kept abreast of everything. I related the Bible to real life. And it wasn't just words. I got involved in social action. I saw the importance of doing as well as talking. Meanwhile I found a spiritual home in a denomination that really suited my temperament, and I have to honestly say I think I did manage to achieve the right kind of balance."

'"And I have to honestly say that, whatever kind of balance you managed to achieve, I never knew you."

'It's a bit frightening, isn't it?' said Gerald softly, after a pause. 'But if what you're asking yourself now is, "How on earth am I ever going to get into heaven if all these amazing characters haven't got a chance?" then just consider one more person who might come along to see Jesus. This time it's Simon Peter, and he's standing by the rail of his laden fishing boat, shading his eyes as he stares towards the distant shore of the lake. The man who stands there next to a recently lit fire was responsible for the huge catch that they've just taken on board, and now, quite suddenly, Peter has realised who it is.

'"Hey, Jesus!" he shouts, "it's me! I'm the one who thought he was being caring and supportive when you seemed determined to die for some reason. But you got really angry and called me Satan and told me to get behind you!

'"And I'm the one who drew his sword when they came for you in the garden that awful night, and would have defended you to the death. But you healed the only one I actually attacked and said that wasn't the kind of help you needed, and after that I didn't know what to do for you so I ran away.

'"Oh, and I'm the one who lied three times about knowing you because I was so embarrassed and scared, and then went and wept and wept because I'd let you down so badly.

'"And do you know what I'm going to do right now? I'm going to jump over the side of this boat and I'm going to run as fast as I can through the water until I get to where you are. And I'm going to do that because I love you and I don't care about any of those other things, and I want to be with you more than anything else in the world and that's all that matters!

'And when Peter gets to the shore and stands before his master, Jesus will look at him and smile and say, "I know you.

You're Peter, and because you truly love me I am going to give you the keys to my Kingdom."

'Learn to love Jesus, and then do what he tells you,' concluded Gerald. 'I have a feeling the rest will look after itself. Amen.'

Held Anne's hand for a moment. Words can get in the way when you want to say really important things.

Invited written questions to be handed in during the interval. Anne sorted through them and chose a few for us to respond to. One of them, written out on the back of a leaflet, said the following:

Dear whichever of you answers this question,

My old mum went into hospital three months ago for tests, and she never came out again because they found she'd got bad cancer and it just raced through her while she was lying there. I've been a Christian for years but mum always pooh-poohed it and said she wasn't interested. Just before she died I told her about Jesus again and said I thought she was going to meet him soon and did she want to ask him to look after her when she got wherever she was going. I thought she was going to react like she always did, but she didn't. She didn't say anything for a while, and then she looked at me and she just said 'Yes, if he'll have me.' That was it. She didn't have the strength to say much more. I was really pleased, but since then I keep worrying. Was it enough? Will I see her again? What about

baptism and proper repentance and all those things? Was it enough? What do you think?
   Love

                    Evelyn

'I'll do that one if you like, Mum,' said Gerald when he saw it.

At the beginning of the second half I did my best to answer one or two questions, and then Gerald said, 'Right, Evelyn's written to us about her mum in hospital.'

He read out the question, then opened his folder.

'The following is for you, Evelyn,' he said, 'hope you find it helpful.'

This is what he read:

> One of the criminals who hangeth there hurleth insults at him: 'Art thou not the Christ? Save thine self and us!'
>
> But the other criminal rebuketh him, saying, 'Do you not fear God, since you are under the same sentence? We are punished justly, for we receiveth what our deeds deserve. But this man has done nothing wrong.'
>
> Then he saith, 'Jesus, wilt thou remember me when that thou comest into thy kingdom?'
>
> Jesus replieth to him, 'Mmm, like to, but er, couple of points. Thou speaketh as though such an simple question might provoketh an simple answer. In fact it dependeth on such issues as thine specific and personal theology, the depth and quality of thine prayer-life in general and the regularity and faithfulness of thine quiet-time in particular. Moving on. As an pretty-well baseline condition, hast thou repented and made confession of thy faith and dost thou have the blessed

assurance that one might reasonably expecteth from a truly born-again believer? Hast thou distinguished in thine own mind between spirituality and religion, and dost thou hold to an eschatological philosophy which embraceth that which hath been divinely revealed by my words and by holy scripture? Speaking of which, hast thou undertaken appropriate exegetical study of those portions of holy writ that are pertinent to thine desire for salvation, oh, and – fancy that I should forgetteth such an crucial one – canst thou offer written or circumstantial evidence that thou hast passed through the waters of baptism in an sound denominational setting?'

The man saith dolefully, 'I'll take that as an 'no' then, shall I?'

'Evelyn, if I was you I'd go and read how Jesus really spoke to that man,' said Gerald. 'I think you'll find it more or less boils down to "Yes".'

Back to our temporary base. Sold *three* of Zak's paintings tonight and might have sold two more if the people who were interested had been able to make their minds up. Can't wait to tell Bernadette when we get back for our day off. In fact, a very successful evening altogether once Leonard and Angels had overcome their panic about exactly the same things as they panicked over last night.

Very relaxed and pleasant feeling back at the hotel, except that I got caught out yet again this evening by one of these stupid someone-at-the-door jokes that Gerald started when he came back home the time before last. Thynn loves them, and

Anne's just as bad. The idea is that you go out and knock on the door or ring the bell, then come back in and tell everyone that someone or something is on the doorstep or just outside the door looking for a place to stay. Then you make an idiotic joke about it. I seem to get caught out every time. Waste of time in my view.

This time it was Leonard who came in to the little hotel sitting-room looking very serious and said, 'Adrian, there are two homeless geologists to see you.'

Put my paper down and half stood up.

'Two homeless – what do they want?'

'They're looking for digs.'

Anne and Gerald fell about.

When they'd subsided, I said, 'Little things please little minds.'

Anne said, 'That reminds me, darling, I must remember to stop off and get some currants for you tomorrow.'

What?

A little later we were treated to Barry's views on the group that Anne and her friend Daphne have started at the church for mothers who just want to get together to talk about problems and generally let off steam. Only about two of them come to our church and the rest are almost certainly not Christians.

'It's going so well!' Anne was saying. 'I'm ever so pleased. I think some of them are talking about how they really feel for the first time in their lives. It's taken a while to get it going because there was quite a lot of suspicion at first, especially as we have the meetings on church property. Some of the mothers couldn't understand why something like this was being offered to them without anyone expecting anything in return, but they love coming now. It's a real break from routine for lots of them. I enjoy it as well. We talk about everything under the sun. Some of it would make you blush, Adrian, I can tell you!'

'May I ask,' said Barry, 'what the ultimate aim of the group is intended to be?'

'There isn't one,' replied Anne promptly, 'having an aim would spoil it. All we want to do is give hassled mums something that's useful to them without any strings attached. I suppose you could call that a sort of aim if you like, but that's all it amounts to.'

Barry said, 'But presumably you put outreach material on the walls and make literature available.'

'And presumably,' chipped in Gerald, 'if the conversation gets round to, say, the price of kitchen rolls, you immediately steer it on to the price that was paid for our salvation on the cross, and then have a little call to the front. That way you could easily process five or six a week, and those who've made a commitment wouldn't need the group any more, because it was only ever intended to be for outreach, so they'd leave, and that would create space for more unsaved mothers to join the following week. You could get through nearly half the Roundwood Estate by Christmas, I would have thought.'

'Exactly!' said Barry.

'Gerald is being facetious, Barry,' said Anne, flushing with annoyance and strength of feeling. 'I wouldn't dream of forcing the conversation round like that, and we certainly aren't thinking of putting anything up on the walls that isn't there already. We want to offer these ladies the love of Jesus on the spot and in practice, not shuttle them off in convoys with a load of theoretical details. If any converting is going to be done I'm quite sure the Holy Spirit is up to the job, and whenever there's a chance for Daphne or me to help in some specific way we're more than happy – overjoyed, in fact – to be allowed to be part of it. What neither of us is going to do is take some sort of benevolently predatory attitude towards people who've often come along to the group precisely because they're tired of being pushed around and told what to do and think at home. We want to love them, not make life more difficult for them.'

Barry was obviously more than a little taken aback by the passion of Anne's speech, but like other people I've met who are super-glued to one idea, there was no question of him parting company with his particular line of thinking.

'If we grant,' he said, 'that there are benefits to these mothers from coming to your group, and that we should, of course, be offering a service to them, we are still left with two indisputable facts. One is that the group meets on church property for an activity run by people from the fellowship, and that the activity in question is partly financed by the use of money collected from members of the church for the general purpose of extending God's Kingdom. You would agree with that, would you not?'

'Yes,' said Anne, quietly and grimly, 'I would.'

'And would you not also agree,' continued Barry, 'that the command of Jesus regarding the preaching of the gospel is very clear in scripture. In the fourth chapter of the gospel according to John, for instance, our Lord tells us that the fields are ripe for harvest, and at the end of Matthew's gospel he commands us to go out and make disciples of all nations. Paul the apostle instructs Timothy to preach the gospel in season and out of season. That is why we are here, to preach the gospel to the unsaved. You would not disagree with that, would you?'

Anne stared down at the floor for what seemed like a very long time after Barry finished speaking, and then she looked up into his face and said, perfectly pleasantly, 'Barry, in meeting you, I have been brought face to face with a phenomenon that is completely new to me. I have never before known anyone who was so completely and utterly right, and at the same time so totally and unequivocally wrong. Everything you say about the Bible and its teaching is accurate and unarguable. Everything you say about real people and real life and the way God actually is in his dealings with sad, confused human beings was born in some other, distant, cold and unfriendly place, and should never have been allowed to live. I think there's a very kind person inside you, Barry, and I really hope and pray you'll teach that person all those Bible verses you know, so that he can use them to bring the love of God to lots and lots of people in the future. I do hope you don't think that I've been rude. Please forgive me if I have been. I'm going to bed now. Goodnight.'

Barry was left blinking rapidly, probably puzzled about whether he was in the right or the wrong. Nobody tried to enlighten him.

Have been sitting up in bed for a while, just watching Anne's face as she sleeps. Felt very proud of her earlier on when she was so direct and certain in what she said to Barry. Why is it some people seem to know what they think as if it had been written down for them, and others – people like me – get pulled and pushed around by the slightest pressure if they're not careful?

I remember a meeting in church once, where one of the items on the agenda was a discussion on the question of whether we should continue to organise our services with the minister at the narrow end of the hall, or swing the whole thing round so that the congregation would be facing the long side wall. I was a strong supporter of the staying-with-the-narrow-end side, and when it was my turn to speak I started off in what I imagined to be true debating style.

'We all know,' I said, in watered down Churchillian style, 'the arguments that are going to be put forward in favour of changing things round. It will be pointed out that people will be closer to each other generally, and there won't be this business of the ones at the back feeling they have no real contact with those who are nearer the front, and vice-versa, because we'll all be able to see each other much more easily. Likewise, someone is bound to say, communion is going to be a lot easier to organise without the business of having to go up through the middle and back down the sides, because more folk will be able to stand up at the front all at the same time than is possible now. No doubt we will also be reminded that the person leading the service or preaching or reading or praying or whatever, will be able to have much more immediate, eye-to-eye communication with the people they're speaking to. Added to that, I'm quite sure that someone will express the admittedly undeniable fact that we would have access to the back rooms through two doors instead of only one, which, in all fairness one has to concede, would make life a great deal easier for the children's workers. And, of course, it will be stressed that, as far as those who are worried about the direction we face are concerned, the chairs face north at the moment, so if we swung them round we'd actually be facing east, which is presumably what they'd want.'

As I paused for breath I noticed Anne staring quizzically at me from a few chairs away.

'So,' I continued rather pompously, 'having said all those things, the fact remains that, in the last analysis – '

I came to an abrupt and slightly bewildered halt at this point, suddenly aware that I couldn't recall any justifications for the other point of view, and that the arguments I had predicted from the swing-it-round contingent had entirely convinced me that they were absolutely right.

Never mind pressure from others. I had talked myself into changing my own mind!

Can't imagine Anne doing that. Nor Gerald, actually. He must have got her genes.

SUNDAY, 23 SEPTEMBER

Funny how you can so quickly lose confidence in your own attitudes. Spent some time over breakfast this morning thinking about Barry's view of the mother's group. Despite the fact that I agreed with everything Anne said last night, the little evangelical imp who lives on my shoulder kept prodding me into wondering if Barry was right after all. Perhaps we shouldn't be squandering resources on something that doesn't produce much in the way of results as far as conversion is concerned. Gerald came in clutching a sheet of paper. Obviously knew exactly what I would be thinking about.

He said, 'Take a look at this, Dad. Another little bit of rewritten scripture. Might help you to  focus your mind.'

Poured another coffee and sat down to read what he'd written.

> Now many seeth them going and recognizeth them, and they hurrieth there

on foot from all the towns and arriveth ahead of them. As he went ashore, he seeth an great crowd; and he had compassion for them, because they were like unto sheep without an shepherd; and he began to teach them many things.

When it grew late, his disciples came unto him and saith, 'This is an deserted place, and the hour is now very late; sendeth them away so that they mayest go into the surrounding country and villages and buyeth something for themselves to eat.'

But he answereth them, 'You giveth them something to eat. I am an preacher, not an mass caterer.'

They saith unto him, 'Are we to go and buyeth two hundred denarii's worth of bread, and giveth it to them to eat?'

And he saith to them, 'An idea striketh me. How many loaves have you? Goeth and see.'

When they had found out, they muttereth, 'It looketh not good. Five, and two small fish.' Then he ordereth them to get all the people to sitteth down in groups on the green grass.

So they sitteth down in groups of hundreds and of fifties. He taketh the five loaves and the two fish, he looketh up to heaven, and blesseth and breaketh the loaves and divided the two fish, and then he whispereth unto his disciples:

'Look, letteth me be absolutely frank about this. Between thou, me and the gatepost to the narrow way, we all know there existeth no such thing as an free lunch. Just take an sheet of papyrus each and have an quick shufti around, keeping thine ears to the ground, and findeth out who among all this bunch of freeloaders hath made an genuine response to the preaching that I have weareth mine self out with for the last couple of hours. No breakthrough equalleth no brunch in my book. Oh, and alloweth not thineselves to be conned by sundry ones who secretly planneth to inhabit the Kingdom of God for just as long as it taketh to eat an fish sandwich.'

And behold it worketh out at an fairly small percentage. And the few who had made an genuine commitment were given bread and fish, and ate and were filled. And afterwards the disciples taketh up twelve baskets full of broken pieces, and the unconverted multitude who remaineth unfed protesteth and waxeth indignant, and saith, ''Ere, we could've had that!'

And the disciples, who sitteth in an circle with the twelve baskets in the middle of them, waggeth their fingers and replieth through mouths stuffed with bread and fish, 'Huh! Thinkest thou we're some kind of open-air McDonald's? Thou heardest the man – no penitence, no picnic. If you don't fear the crunch, don't expect the lunch.'

And behold, those who had eaten not departeth, grumbling, to the surrounding country and villages to buy food for themselves, and they saith things like unto, 'Wish I'd never come now' and 'Thinkest thou I shall goeth out of my way to listeneth to him again? Well, holdest not thine breath if thou do!' And the last to leave saith, 'What an pooey swiz!'

And behold, afterwards Jesus saith unto the disciples, 'Err, small point, lads, whoever recordeth this – no need to mention the ones that eateth not. It spoileth the image, if thou getteth mine drift . . .'

Took Gerald's point. Funny thing about these scripture rewrites of his is that they always make me want to go back and read the original as if I'd never seen it before. Sometimes think the Bible's a bit like the pictures on my living-room wall. I get so used to them that I stop looking properly at them, and then when someone points one out I remember why I loved it enough to want to live with it. Shared this insight with Anne when she came in for her breakfast.

She said, 'I feel exactly the same about you, darling.'

We all popped into the local Anglican church, St Brandon's, for the morning service. Turned out to be communion. Anne and I love the Anglican communion.

To our surprise the vicar turned out to be Vladimir Spool, who used to be the minister in charge of St Dermot's, the Anglican church just up the road from where we live. At the time when we knew him Vladimir invariably reacted to anything I said as though it was amazingly clever, and, perhaps because of that, he had once managed to persuade me to take on the task of doing a children's address at his church one Sunday.

Despite the fact that, due to my own abject, cringing fear, I scared the children nearly to death with my dreadful talk, he insisted that the little ones had been greatly challenged by my message, and expressed his view that a lesson was far more likely to lodge in tiny minds when it came wrapped up in a well told story. The truth was that I barely escaped being lynched by a posse of parents who objected strongly to the effect that my very poor but terrifying story might have had on the tiny minds of their children.

Enjoyed the service today very much, not least because Reverend Spool was as innocently complicated in most of his practical announcements as he had ever been. It began at the very beginning when we nearly drowned in books and pamphlets and leaflets and things stuffed into the wooden slot in front of us.

Reverend Spool said, 'Welcome, everybody, and a very special welcome to any visitors who are here for the first time. For their benefit and to simplify matters I should explain that we use the yellow service card in the blue folder at the back of the green hymnbook in conjunction with the orange leaflet attached to the pink information sheet inside the brown pew Bible.'

Just about got it sorted out by the time the service ended.

Decided to stay for coffee and say hello to Vladimir.

He appeared to be ecstatically happy to meet me again, a little like Mabilene in Los Angeles, except that, in Vladimir's case, I am quite sure that the pleasure was totally genuine.

'Yes, well, no, but – goodness me, what a treat and a pleasure!' he enthused as I introduced everyone. 'May I be bold enough to ask what brings you and your attractive wife and your charming son and your very dear and lovely friends to this humble part of the world?'

'Oh,' I said, automatically adopting the modest tones that I had always used in the past with Vladimir, knowing that my most inane burblings were bound to be treated as if they were gems of profound wisdom, 'it's a sort of – well, a sort of short tour that we're doing. Gerald and I speak a bit, and Angels dances, and Leonard looks after the, er, practical side, and Anne does all sorts of things. It's a – it's a sort of tour,' I ended lamely.

'A *tour*!' gasped Vladimir in awestruck tones. 'No, well, goodness me, yes! That is quite *wonderful*! A tour! You are on a *tour*!'

'Yes,' I confirmed wretchedly, 'it's a tour.'

'And you are speaking to people on your tour! Well, yes, but no, of course – you will not recall this, Anne, my dear, as I don't believe you were actually present, but Adrian came to

St Dermot's when I was the priest in charge there and delivered a talk to our small children that was – well, it was
absolutely *riveting*. They were gripped, positively *gripped* by
the power of your husband's vivid imagery and the profound
meaning of his tale. I can see those little faces and bodies in my
mind's eye now. It was as if those little people were frozen into
immobility by the sheer pleasure of listening.'

He turned to beam at Gerald.

'You were there, young man. I am right, am I not?'

'Oh, yes,' said Gerald. 'You're right, Reverend Spool, they
were definitely frozen. No doubt about that.'

'Anyway,' I interrupted hastily, 'how are you,
Vladimir? What are you up to at the moment?'

The vicar became thoughtful.

'No, well, actually, yes, we have a meeting in
just a few minutes from now to discuss our newly formed
young people's group. The two main items on the agenda are
the selection of a name for the group and some discussion as to
how their excesses might be significantly curbed.'

'Bit wild, are they?' enquired Gerald.

'They are *wonderful* young people,' said Vladimir, his face
lighting up again, 'with a very real sense of immanent spirituality and a genuine beauty of spirit, but one must acknowledge
that at their initial gathering they bound and gagged our youth
worker, destroyed much of our new hall kitchen and purloined
the majority of our electrical appliances, presumably in order
to sell them on. So, you will understand, for some there is that
tinge of negative behaviour associated with the situation.'

'Goodness me!' said Anne. 'And did you say you're meeting
to think of a name for the group?'

'Well, that was certainly the plan before these unfortunate happenings,' said Vladimir sadly, 'but it may well be that there will be some adjustment to our agenda in the circumstances.'

'How about calling them Satan's Little Helpers?' offered Gerald.

Vladimir failed to register this helpful suggestion.

'I had wondered,' he said tentatively, 'if the name "Puma" might be a fitting one. You see, our lovely young people are in that marvellous stage between puberty and maturity, and such a title would rather fascinatingly reflect that interestingly mixed state, would it not? Puma! Do you see?'

We were saved from having to respond to this truly appalling suggestion by the fact that Vladimir, happening to glance at his watch, realised that he had to go to his meeting. In the act of turning to go, however, he stopped abruptly, looked at me, and lit up like a beacon, as if with some new inspiration.

'I suppose, Adrian,' he said excitedly, 'there is no chance that you would still be in the area on Friday evening. Your communication skills might be just the thing to help our young people to begin realising their enormous potential!'

My throat went dry and my stomach turned a double somersault. Nothing on this earth outside a direct order from God written on the wall and witnessed by hundreds would have persuaded me to give Vladimir's gang of young thugs an excuse to jeer at everything I said, mug me in the toilets and leave my bleeding body to be stretchered off to the nearest Accident and Emergency unit if and when it was discovered in the morning. Fortunately, I didn't have to lie. We would be long gone by Friday. Thank you, God!

Vladimir was disappointed, but we parted with lots of beaming and waving and good wishes. I wiped my brow as he passed from view.

'Narrow escape, eh, Dad?' said Gerald. 'Pity, really. You might have been just what those little Pumas needed. And Vladimir would have thought you were wonderful whatever you did. Actually, I was pretty sure that God was telling me you should have said yes to Vladimir.'

My heart nearly failed me.

'You're not serious, are you?'

'No,' said Gerald, 'I'm not.'

Really thought Thynn had suffered some sort of fit or seizure in the van this afternoon.

It happened just before we reached our hotel when Barry, who seems to be getting more and more frustrated about Gerald's challenge, said that he'd worked out what the answer was.

'In the eighteenth verse of the twenty-second chapter of Luke's gospel,' he said, 'the Lord informed his disciples that he would not drink wine until the Kingdom of God had been established. Clearly, through these words he was conveying some other message, as it cannot possibly be the case that the presence of alcohol would be tolerated in the realms of glory. We know – '

It was at this point that Barry was interrupted by a sort of animal cry from Leonard, who followed it up by gasping, 'Not that verse! Don't tell me that verse isn't true! It's the only thing that keeps me going sometimes – the thought that if he could wait, so can I. Don't tell me it isn't true, please . . .'

Chaos for a while with Anne and Angels comforting Leonard and Barry wanting to know what he'd said that was so upsetting, and me trying to explain about Leonard's drinking problem without Leonard hearing.

When peace had finally returned, Gerald grinned, leaned over and whispered in Barry's ear, 'Anyway – you're wrong!'

Lots to write about tonight.

Difficult to understand why some people ask me to come and speak at their churches at all.

Anne went off to do an early evening children's meeting at the local Anglican centre, while the rest of us drove round to Witton Baptist church to speak on the subject 'What if I've been wounded?' Arrived outside the building to find that either vandals or the wind or general wear and tear or God or the devil had caused one of the wooden letters announcing the name of the church to drop off the wall. The sign now read:

WITTON BA TIST CHURCH

Began my talk by pointing out that, judging by the sign out-side, someone had been taking the P out of the Baptists as usual. This remark greeted with a sort of relieved chuckle by the majority of the audience, and grim silence by a few of the rest.

Realised, on looking around at the congregation and think-ing about the title of the talk I'd been asked to give, that most of the people there wouldn't be feeling very wonderful about themselves or what was happening in their lives. Not an occasion for telling people off.

Talked about how tough things had been for Anne and me sometimes, and how much we'd failed and still do fail. How, when things are really dark, Jesus is just the faintest of faint nightlights – if that, and you have to strain your eyes to see him and believe that he really is still there. Said a bit about the relief of giving up the effort involved in trying to be what other people said we should be, and how nice it was to be like Mary sitting at the feet of Jesus, just enjoying being there with him, instead of fretting and worrying about getting a thousand unnecessary things done.

Set out to lighten the atmosphere a bit by telling the true story of a man called Henry Rung, who was a member of our church at home until his death a few years ago. Henry was a very small, quite elderly widower with just a wisp of white hair and almost no teeth, who did occasional gardening for people in the church. After a day's work in our garden he'd obviously developed an intense crush on Anne, and he started coming round to our house on every pretext under the sun. It could be gifts of flowers and plants from his own garden, bits of news about other church members or questions about how to cook such and such a meal. Anne felt sorry for this lonely old man who just stood and gazed at her like a love-sick schoolboy every time she swam into his view, and she was as kind to him as she always is to everyone else, but she did start to get fed-up with his constant appearances.

Gerald, on the other hand, loved every moment of it. He would come through after answering the door, wink extravagantly and suggestively at his mother, and say, 'Fix your hair, Mum, Henry Rung's here. It's you he wants, and he won't take no for an answer!'

Blinded by his teenage-style, septuagenarian passion, Henry hardly seemed to register my existence at all. Never have much enjoyed not existing.

Finally goaded into deciding to have a quiet word with Henry after Gerald fooled me with a bit of his usual nonsense. Sat down very gravely with me one afternoon when Anne was out and said he had a question to ask.

'Yes?' I said.

'Actually, it's about Henry Rung. There's a problem.'

Wondered, for one wild, foolish moment, if Gerald was about to tell me that Anne and Henry had packed two little bags and run away together to some exotic South American city. A moment's reflection suggested that this was a less than likely scenario.

'What sort of problem?'

'I don't want to be morbid, Dad, but – well, suppose you died very suddenly in the near future. Heaven forbid, of *course*, but supposing you did.'

'All right, supposing I did. What would that have to do with Henry Rung?'

'Well,' continued Gerald seriously, 'suppose that after – you know – a decent interval, Mum was so desolated and lonely that she decided to seek happiness in the arms of Henry Rung – '

'What!'

Gerald spread his arms.

'Stranger things have been known, Dad. You can't predict anything where feelings are concerned, can you? Loneliness has been known to do some very funny things to people. Anyway, my question is this.'

'Yes, Gerald,' I said, sensing that I was about to hear something extremely silly, but also knowing I was just short of being absolutely sure, 'what is your question?'

'Right, this is it. If mum marries Mr Rung and becomes Mrs Rung, will that mean that Henry is my stepladder?'

I suppose you can't clip your grown-up son round the ear, can you?

The experience of being lured into this ludicrous cul-de-sac of flippancy would indeed have spurred me on to doing something about Henry's constant visiting, except that a couple of days later we heard that the old fellow had died quite suddenly and unexpectedly. We all went to his funeral and felt very sad, especially when we pictured him arriving in heaven and getting an eternal ear-bashing from his previously departed Dora for pestering Anne so much.

Finished my talk by reminding everybody that Christians know a secret that the rest of the world doesn't. Wherever there's a crucifixion there can be a resurrection. If you're one of the wounded, I told them, hang on in there and wait for God to rescue you, and we'll all compare notes one day in heaven.

Very positive reaction from most of the audience, who loved the dance that Angels performed for them after I'd spoken, and seemed to have got more and more relaxed and cheerful as the evening went on. But at the end, after the applause had died down, Dave Campbell (why are they always called Dave Campbell?), the person who had invited me to come, and who had also given me the title of my talk, got up from his seat on the front row and glided to the microphone. Spoke in one of those soupy, iron-tonsils-in-the-velvet-throat voices that, in the past, have sometimes made me want to run screaming into the night.

'I'm sure everyone here would like to thank Adrian for his very entertaining talk, and of course we all know that the Lord Jesus Christ has promised to come into our hearts if we simply ask him. Whatever might be clouding our minds tonight, he will certainly meet the need in us. The Lord is mighty and swift to deal with those problems that affect our walk with him. Oh, friends, if we will but reach out to him in our affliction he will be faithful and just in reaching out to us. Isaiah tells us the word that goes out from his mouth will not return to him empty. And all God's people said – ?'

A smattering of God's people muttered a miserable, guilt-laden 'Amen', but the atmosphere was ruined. Dave Campbell's fear that I might not have dotted the i's and crossed the t's of the gospel message seemed to have taken them right back to the place where they had started. Most of those people knew all about asking Jesus into their hearts. What they wanted more than anything else in the world was to get things right and overcome the feelings of pain and confusion that were crippling their lives. The sort of teaching that tells you B will definitely happen if only you do A is likely to produce failure and guilt if the formula doesn't happen to work for you. Anne and Gerald and I know only too well that God sometimes takes a route through H to get from A to B, and he might even stop off at J and X on the way, hanging around long enough to find out how I and K and W and Y and the rest of the neighbours are getting along.

Left quickly with the others at the end instead of stopping to talk and pray with people. Wished I hadn't. Shows how fragile I am. Dave Campbell's prayer made me feel all embarrassed and silly.

Felt really guilty and depressed by the time I got back to the hotel. A bit cheered up by Anne telling me that she could see how I must have felt. I never know whether Anne's going to tell me off or be sympathetic. I suppose she's a bit like God in that respect.

Further cheered on hearing about the children's meeting from Anne. She said that one little girl, obviously thinking about the amount of cutting and sticking and colouring that goes on in the junior church, joined in with one of the choruses, singing at the top of her voice, 'Come on, let's sellotape . . . !'

Hearing this, Thynn said that when he was a little boy he had wondered why everyone had to keep asking God to send plums to the queen.

We all stared.

He said, 'You see, I thought when we sang the national anthem it said, "Send her victorias", and I knew mother sometimes bought Victoria plums along at the shop, so I thought that was what we were asking God to send her. I used to wonder what her majesty did with all those tons and tons of plums that must have kept arriving every time the national anthem was sung. I reckoned she and the Duke of Edinburgh had to have pies every day and lots and lots of jam.'

Couldn't help smiling as I remembered how, when I directed a play at the church, I had found it almost impossible to unravel Leonard's fixed belief that it was traditional for stage prompters to wear a soldier's uniform. That was all because of a childhood misunderstanding as well, and in fact I never did quite unravel it as far as Leonard himself was concerned. He must have been the only person in the history of the theatre to dress as a French colonial officer in order to prompt the actors from a position where the audience would never see him.

'The other thing I didn't understand when I was very little,' said Thynn, 'was why Jesus and the disciples had to take a little baby girl around with them everywhere they went.'

Short, dazed silence.

'You know,' said Gerald slowly, reflectively and with a sort of profound relish, 'I simply cannot wait to hear why you thought they had to take a baby girl around with them. In fact, that's what I like about you, Leonard. You say something like that and we all wait in what I can only describe as a state of *awe* to see how random pieces of the universe will come flying together to make unexpected sense of a statement that, on the face of it, means absolutely nothing at all.'

'Well, thank you, Gerald, for your faith in me.'

'Don't mention it, Leonard. Just tell us why you thought Jesus and the disciples took a baby girl around with them. Then I can die happy.'

'Well, someone read something in church one day about them being accompanied by Judith's carry-cot. And I thought – '

Rest of Leonard's explanation was drowned by laughter. When we'd settled down a bit, Anne said, 'What about you,

Angels? Was there anything you thought when you were little that turned out to be wrong when you were older?'

We all looked at Angels. Amazing how she's relaxed since we first met her. All those long obscure speeches seem to have become quite unnecessary now.

Funny little painful pause, then quite unexpectedly Angels' big eyes brimmed with tears and she said, in a little trembly voice, 'Thought I would be happy.'

Anne moved round to sit beside Angels and put an arm around her shoulders. Leonard looked on aghast, twisting his hands together in anguish.

'But, Angels, sweetheart,' said Anne, 'whatever's happened in the past, you've got Leonard now, and we're all very fond of you. You're our friend and we love having you with us.' She turned to Gerald and I. 'Don't we?'

'Not half!' said Gerald, 'I think you're a smasher.'

Never been very good at this sort of thing. Feelings stick in my gullet, and tend to come out all stiff and cold like a frozen chicken. I could easily have ended up saying something along the lines of: 'I would like to formally endorse the sentiments expressed previously by my wife and extend my very best wishes for your future happiness.'

I didn't, thank God! Just nodded and smiled as warmly as I could.

'Thing is,' said Angels, still in that shaky little voice, 'I can't ever be like the rest of you, be a – a Christian, I mean.'

'Why not?' asked Gerald very quietly.

Angels flicked a glance at Leonard before answering.

'I've done – things. Bad things. Mostly when I was dancing for a living and travelling around all over the place. I've done

some very silly, very bad things in my life. They've made me
very weak and – and sort of worn out. I don't see how God
could want me, not if he's seen what I've done. Do you think
he has seen what I've done?'

'Oh, yes,' said Gerald, 'he doesn't miss a thing – but,
Angels, look, this is very bad news indeed.'

Angels opened her eyes very wide.

'Do you mean that I can't be with you or – '

'Oh, no, not at all! No, what I meant by the bad news was
that none of us can be Christians either.'

'What Gerald is trying to say in his usual convoluted way,'
said Anne, giving Angels' shoulders a squeeze and smiling, 'is
that none of us could be Christians if God was going to judge
us by the things that we've done. We've all made mistakes.
Little things, big things, in one way it doesn't really matter
whether it's murder or not helping with the washing-up. The
biggest and most important mistake any of us can make is finding out that God loves us like the very best father we can imagine, and that he wants us to come home to him and be close to
him, and then doing nothing about it.'

'My daddy loved me,' said Angels softly.

'Okay, well, you imagine this, then. Your dad says to you,
"Angela, I really love you, please give me a cuddle." And you
turn round to him and say, "No, I'm not going to cuddle you.
I know you don't love me. I was naughty five times last week,
so you can't love me".'

Two huge tears rolled out of Angels' eyes and trickled down
into her dessert bowl.

'I wouldn't have said that to my dad. He really, really
loved me.'

'God loves you even more than your dad did,' said Anne, 'and I'm pretty sure he would love to give you a cuddle.' She looked up. 'Adrian and Gerald, why don't you leave Leonard and Angels and I to have a chat, and we'll see you later.'

Barry went off to his room, while Gerald and I retired to the bar and sat over a couple of brandies.

Thought for a bit and said, 'How did your mother remember in the middle of all that talking that her dad would have called her Angela, and not Angels?'

'That's mum for you,' said Gerald, chuckling gently, 'she usually gets it right, doesn't she? Wish I could take her back to the parish with me.'

Companionable pause, then I said, in as casual a tone as I could manage, 'So, just as a matter of interest, Gerald, when you look back is there much in your life that you wish – well, that you're really ashamed of?'

'Me? Ooh, let me see now.' He stared at the ceiling for a moment or two. 'Mm, there was one thing a couple of us did when we were students that I can't even think about without either feeling very ashamed or laughing out loud – or both. Never told you or mum at the time, of course.'

'Go on, then,' I said, 'spill the beans.'

'Right. Sure you want to hear this?'

''Course!'

'Okay, well, you remember the second-floor flat with the fancy balcony that my friend Jeff and I had in that nice little square with the pretty gardens in the middle, down in Southampton?'

'Do I remember? How could I forget? I nearly did my back in carting stuff up to the second floor when you first moved in. There was an awful moment on the stairs when it felt as if one of those blasted tapering table-legs had deliberately gone in the front of me, come out the back of me and spiked itself into the wall behind me. I thought I might be doomed to spend the rest of my life impaled into the angle of the stairs, and have to be fed bits and pieces over the edge of the – '

'Anyway, there was a tall, thin, beaky-nosed elderly bloke called Dunmall living in the flat below who set out from the very first day we moved in to make life uncomfortable for us.'

'Yes, I vaguely remember you mentioning him. Didn't he go on at you about making too much noise?'

'That's right. In fact, that very day you came and helped, not long after we finished the Chinese takeaway and you and mum had gone, he came up and banged on our door and said that we'd sounded like a herd of crazed rhinoceroses crashing about over his head, and he hoped that things would be different in the future. Well, I don't know how well you remember Jeff, but his flippancy made me look like a mummified undertaker. He reacted as if this bloke had welcomed us with open arms, and he kept a really straight face. He said something along the lines of: "Well, that is very kind of you, and Gerald and I are just as pleased to get here as you are to see us arrive. And can we just say what a difference it makes to get a really warm welcome like this? Thank you so much for going out of your way to make a difficult day just that little bit easier."

'Complete waste of time, of course. Mr Dunmall turned out to be the sort of person who's incapable of understanding anything you say to him if it isn't something he's expecting to hear.

He plagued our lives after that. We did go out of our way to avoid making unnecessary noise, tip-toeing around like ghosts when it was late and taking ages over shutting doors, that sort of thing. We did our best. We even invited him in for coffee and stuff a couple of times to try to make friends, but nothing made any real difference. We were students, you see, so as far as he was concerned, we obviously had to be into all sorts of horrible things. It was a lovely flat, and we had a great time there, but there was always this underlying, grinding tension, so, when we left – well, we just thought it would be nice to give Mr Dunmall a little leaving present.'

'That was very nice of you in the circumstances.'

'Trust me, it wasn't.'

'Oh.'

'No, what we did was this. We got a cardboard box and put a few things in it with the lid open, then on the day that we left we gave the box to Mr Dunmall and told him it had been dropped off by the person who was coming to take over our flat a few days later. We asked him if he would mind looking after it until the new tenant came to collect it. Well, he wasn't all that keen, of course, but we had a pretty good idea that he'd be very curious about the contents of the box, so we just left it with him. Finally we cleared off with the last of our stuff a bit later after Jeff had told him how grateful we were for his forbearance and co-operation during the time we'd been there, and how much we appreciated the give and take that had made our relationship such a special one.' Gerald threw his head back and laughed suddenly. 'That Jeff really was a beggar, you know. He almost had me believing his rubbish for a moment.'

'So what was in the box?'

'Oh, just a few things to help Mr Dunmall look forward to meeting his new neighbours. Let me think. There was a thick file, for instance, sealed, but with a very convincingly printed label on the front saying in big red capital letters "GAY RAVE NEWS 1–20". And then there was a music book that we'd bought in town that was called "Violin for Absolute Beginners". What else did we put in? Ah, yes, there was one of those practical "how to" books. This one was about how to throw a successful party for a large number of people in a limited space. We popped a deflated basketball in there just to stimulate his imagination, and a couple of back-issues of a magazine called "Hi-fi Monthly". I think we even put a hammer and some six-inch nails in the box as well. Oh, I nearly forgot, Jeff found an old pair of tap-shoes in a charity shop, so we bunged those in as well. We put a lot of thought and time and effort into that little collection, I can tell you. Later on we sat over a drink and just enjoyed trying to imagine Mr Dunmall's face as he picked through that lot.'

'Sweet revenge, eh?'

'Well, yes, I must admit that it felt pretty good, the idea of Mr Dunmall looking forward to the evening when there'd be a huge and rowdy party in the room over his head, with some-one playing the violin excruciatingly badly in the background, someone else bouncing a basketball around all over the floor, the hi-fi up at full volume, the old six-inch nails being bashed into the wall, and, just to make the evening complete, a fre-netic tap-dance going on into the early hours of the morning. I do feel guilty when I look back now, though. I mean, it wasn't exactly textbook outreach, was it? And we never did find out what happened when the new tenants arrived and were presented with what was supposed to be their box. Gosh, just imagine that! To be honest, I think our dearest wish at the time was that someone would come to visit Mr Dunmall and spot his "Gay Rave News" folder sitting in the corner.' He shook his head. 'You don't think as much when you're younger, do you? I mean, suppose Mr Dunmall walked into my church one Sunday and saw me standing up the front. He'd probably turn round and walk straight out. Now that would be a bit of a tragedy.'

Gerald and I nodded gravely at one another for several seconds, and then, as though someone had pressed a switch, we both burst into laughter at exactly the same time.

It's a problem I've often noticed in the past. Being a Christian would be a lot easier if things were more black and white. Finding the wrong things funny is a good example. If off-colour jokes and situations never made you laugh there wouldn't be a problem.

Listening to Gerald brought back memories of an occasion when I went away to the west country on my own to speak at a church, and when I arrived all the people involved in the evening were taking a break, sitting on chairs in a little circle in the church hall drinking cups of tea and chatting. At the precise moment when I walked through the door a very erect, grey-faced, almost funereal looking man with a thin, tapering head uttered the following graphic words:

'So, the clinic was able to go ahead as planned, but they had to tie our clappers up.'

They all noticed that I'd come in at that point, and one or two got up to greet me and someone went and poured me a cup of tea, so it wasn't until we were all settled back into the circle once more that they carried on with their conversation. But it had passed beyond the clappers by then, and I was left wondering what on earth that very serious man had been talking about. Not only that, but something about his grave delivery of those extraordinary words had tickled my sense of humour so much that I was finding it quite difficult to control myself. It was when I suddenly emitted a guffaw on hearing that the lady who had been going to collect the tickets was unwell and couldn't do it, that I realised I would have to ask the question or look even more of a heartless loony than I did already.

'I'm sorry,' I said, 'I wasn't laughing about poor Mrs Jennings. Honestly, I wasn't. I hope she gets well very soon. No, it was just that I haven't been able to stop thinking about what the fellow over there was saying as I came into the hall just now.'

Eight pairs of eyes looked innocently and enquiringly at me. I came close to chickening out. Perhaps I'd imagined the whole thing. How, I asked myself, could such an upright, thin-headed man possibly have produced that particular collection of words?

'Mr Salmons, do you mean?' said one of the ladies, indicating the gentleman in question with a little wave of her hand.

'Er, yes,' I replied, 'that's right, it was Mr Salmons.'

'What did he say?' enquired a fluffy haired little lady with bright blue eyes who looked as if she had never thought, done, said or witnessed anything remotely impure since the day of her birth.

'Well – '

I broke off and tried to produce a matey chuckle expressing the fact that we were all friendly men and women of the world who would be able to see the funny side of certain slightly vulgar things even though we stood for the same high standards of decency and respectability.

'Just as I walked through the door,' I said, 'Mr Salmons was saying – I think he was saying – that the clinic went ahead as planned, but they had to have their clappers tied up.'

I waited. Surely, just one of the people in this circle of innocence would be able to see how strange that must have sounded to someone walking into the situation? I looked for a glimmer of amusement in their faces. Nothing. In the country of the pure, the man with the vulgar streak is an idiot.

'That is quite correct,' said Mr Salmons in his dry, dispassionate voice. 'The person who came to lead our bell ringing clinic was delayed, and by the time we started it was considered too late to trouble our neighbours with the sound of bells, so we agreed to go through the motions of various exercises, but with our clappers tied, so as not to cause offence.'

Nods of confirmation from around the circle.

'Ah,' I said feebly, 'that explains it. Your clappers tied so as not to cause offence. Thank you very much for, er – for explaining it. Thank you.'

From that point on the group seemed to regard me as being amiable but rather surprisingly dim-witted. Everything was explained to me in slightly more detail than was absolutely necessary, and trouble was taken to ensure that I never had to find anything for myself. They were all very kind and attentive, but I finished the evening feeling like a fool with a dark secret. I resolved that in future I would think very carefully before asking questions that I did not actually need to have answered.

Asked Anne how it had gone with Angels when I got back to my room.

'Oh, Adrian,' she said, 'she's such a sweet person, and so sure that she's worth nothing. I know she and Leonard have only known each other a little while, but wouldn't it be wonderful if they did stay together? Poor Leonard's all twitchy about whether or not she's going to become a Christian.'

'Do you think she will?'

'I think if we keep on praying for her, she might. It would be a good idea to pray for her now, wouldn't it?'

'Yes.'

So we did.

MONDAY, 24 SEPTEMBER

Quite a fierce debate in the van on the way home early this morning about how much God is in charge of every part of our lives. Angels said that she would love to think that God really does get involved with every tiny detail of what happens to us, but that when you looked around at all the horrible things that were happening in the world it was very difficult to believe.

Barry said, 'Not to Christians, though,' and nearly got drowned in waves of protests from the others. Everyone seemed to have at least one story about something incredibly nasty that had happened to a Christian. Barry battled back to the surface eventually and said, 'But the Bible spells it out very clearly. Not a single sparrow falls to the ground without the Father knowing about it.'

'Yes,' said Anne seriously, 'he knows all about it, but they still fall to the ground, don't they, Barry? Jesus never promised that we would avoid problems, just

that he would be with us in the middle of them. Terrible things do happen to Christians all the time. Do you remember the lady at that meeting we went to, Adrian, who said that tens of thousands of Christians are being martyred every year in different places round the world? Lots of little sparrows fluttering to the ground, and not a lot of miracle rescues as far as we know. I just thank God that he knows them and they'll be allowed to get their broken wings working somewhere else.'

Silence for a moment or two, then Barry said, 'Yes, but you must admit, often when you look back at what's happened to you, you can see the sense of it. You know, you can tell what the over-all plan really was. I was talking to a lady the other day who lost her small son in a road accident, and then, just a couple of months later, her grandmother got seriously ill and had to be nursed and looked after twenty-four hours a day until she died. This lady said she could see now that if she'd still had her son it would have been impossible to look after her granny. So you see, looking back at what had happened there was a reason – a pattern.'

Nobody spoke as we all contemplated this dismal picture of a God who, like some omnipotent, unscrupulous organiser of a time-table of care facilities, saw fit to arrange the death of a little boy so that an awkward upcoming vacancy could be filled.

'I should think that makes God weep,' said Anne at last.

'What?' said Barry.

'Oh, you know, the thought of this lady, huddled at the end of her sad little off-shoot from the main path, clutching tightly on to that pathetically thin rationalisation and struggling to accept that this really is as good as it gets. Oh, I know that what you say is true sometimes, Barry, but it so often seems to be just another of those very human devices we use to avoid facing the fact that, in the end, we either trust God or we don't. I'm willing to follow you unconditionally – as long as it's on my terms. That's what most of us are really saying to God, isn't it?'

Anne is amazing sometimes.

'Mm, I don't know though, Mum, things do sometimes seem different in retrospect,' said Gerald in that ominously grave tone of his.

Braced myself.

'The other day, for instance, I had a horrible experience. I was just walking quietly down the road when suddenly the earth cracked open, there was the sound of a mighty rushing wind, huge horsemen on gigantic steeds appeared among the clouds, a great darkness fell over the land and a shining throne descended from the sky, on which sat a figure dressed in white, holding a sword and shining like the sun. Well, you know how it is, at the time it seemed like the end of the world, but looking back . . .'

One of the ways in which Gerald hasn't changed at all is his tendency to go on squeezing and bashing away at a joke or an argument until there isn't a single drop left in it. Wouldn't be so bad only the others seem to really enjoy joining in once he gets going. Ridiculous example this morning when we were only about a mile from home.

I said, 'Shall we turn right here and go through the estate, or shall we wait until we get to the Garden Centre and go down to the town from there?'

Gerald said, incredulously, 'Down? You don't go *down* to the town from the Garden Centre. You go *up*. Everyone who lives up this end says, 'I'm just going up to town. That's what you do. You go *up* to town. '

'Ah-hah!' I replied, 'You just said "Everyone who lives *up* this end". How can they talk about going *up* to town if they're already "*up*" this end before they start?'

'Oh, that's just an expression!' said Gerald. 'They say they live *up* this end of town and then when they actually go into town they talk about going up to town because that's what everybody's always said. You go *up* to town.' He turned to the others. 'Don't you go up from here?'

All nodded and said things with 'up' in italics.

Anne said, 'Besides which, darling, the road does actually go uphill for almost the whole way from the Garden Centre to the town.'

'Up*hill*? No it does *not*!' I protested scornfully. 'It's nearly all down hill. That's why it makes so much more sense to talk about going down to town.'

Chorus of mocking laughter from the others.

'Well,' I said, 'we shall soon see, shan't we?'

Funny how your memory lets you down. After we turned right there was a long steep hill going upwards before the short downhill bit that was stuck in my mind. At this point, in my view, the comments started to get childish and silly.

As we started to climb the hill, Gerald said, 'Well, looks as if dad was dead right after all. I'd better get into first gear and keep my foot on the brake. Here we go, down, down, down into the very bowels of the earth, corkscrewing our way towards that dark uncharted world in the middle of the planet. You all right, Mum?'

'Yes, fine, just a spot of vertigo,' said Anne. 'I never have been able to look down from a great height without feeling sick and giddy.'

'It's a bit like the end of *Titanic*, isn't it,' said Angels, as we continued to toil up the hill, 'when the ship goes up on its end and people are falling hundreds of feet down into the water. We'd all better hold on tight!'

'The maelstrom awaits!!' cried Gerald, like someone bawling over the noise of the music in the climax of a bad 'B' movie with Doug McClure in it. 'Boy, it's getting hot! We can't be far from the molten core at the centre of the earth!'

When Leonard started speaking in an Australian accent 'so that he'd be sure to fit in when we arrive', I decided that enough was enough.

'All right, all right! Very funny, I don't think! We're travelling uphill on our way to the bit where you go down on your way up to town, and I don't care any more. I give up.'

'Give up? Don't you mean *down*, Dad?'

Day off!

Dropped in on Bernadette just after we got back. Told her how much people had enjoyed Zak's paintings, and gave her the money for the three that have already been sold. She shed a little tear, and told me what pleasure it had been giving her to think of her husband's pictures travelling along with us over the last three days. Almost as if he was with us himself, she said. Had a quick cup of tea, gave her a little kiss on the cheek and left.

Got home and flopped in the kitchen to take stock. Couple of things on my mind. One is that there are all sorts of areas in my life where I'm pretty well incompetent. Found myself wishing I could paint like Zak, but I'm not even that good at managing practical things, let alone being artistic. Must find a way of tackling one or two of these real shortcomings.

Also found myself reflecting this morning that so far I've really enjoyed our little tour except for negative things that have been repeated every single time we've arrived at a venue where we're all doing things together. One is Angels and the space she needs to do her dances, and the other is Thynn and his screen and his projector and his slides.

I may be wrong, but I have a feeling that if we arrived in the Gobi desert and I told Angels that she was able to use the entire expanse of sand in any way she wished, she would tell me that there was a claustrophobic feel about the setting that made it difficult if not impossible for her to express herself with true artistic freedom. I understand that it's sheer fear making her react like this, but it does get a bit wearing after a while.

Think I'll go and ask Anne what she thinks before I write any more.

I've asked Anne what she thinks.

I said, 'Maybe it would be better if we didn't bother with an audience. We could just clear all the chairs out and let Angels dance in the space that's left, and we'll all watch.'

Anne said, 'Don't be silly, darling, we're dealing with someone who's being very brave. Getting up to dance in these places

136

is like climbing a steep mountain for Angels every single time. I think she's doing remarkably well. Let's just put up with the nerves and keep on encouraging her.'

Yes, well, that's exactly the answer I would have given to myself if I'd asked me what I thought about what I was thinking – if you see what I mean.

Didn't mention how I was feeling about Thynn.

I really am extremely fond of Leonard, but I have to confess there are times when I think of him as a prime candidate for an imaginary giant blender into which I place people like that pompous little man on television who talks about antiques, and a lady down the road from us who, for as long as I can remember, has looked disapprovingly at me every time we've met, and occasional fit young men with long upper bodies and peaked caps turned backwards who play tennis ferociously on the next court to me and make me feel old and silly. Doesn't sound terribly Christian on the face of it, does it? I have tried to get rid of that blender, but it keeps on floating back into my mind.

The trouble with Thynn on this tour is that he doesn't seem to learn anything from one event to the next. Every single time he walks into a new venue he flies into a twittering panic and starts doing a sort of Forrest Gump circular run round the edge of the church or hall, shouting about the fact that it isn't going to be possible to find anywhere that will allow an eight-foot throw between the projector and the screen. Then, after I've found a way to make that possible and he's managed yet again to subdue the malevolent spirit that seems to inhabit that huge screen and its frame and turn it into a vast sail whenever you try to stick it up somewhere, the moment arrives for mixing up the slides in the carousel and making sure that they go into their little slots in entirely the wrong order.

To be fair, it isn't just Leonard. There really is something uncanny about the way those slides jumble themselves up, no matter how carefully you put them in. On that first evening, for instance, my question to the audience about God's ultimate aim for each one of us was accompanied by a close-up of dead bodies in a war zone. Shortly afterwards I began to talk about the Holy Spirit looking beyond our exteriors and seeing us as we will one day appear to God. According to the slide that Thynn threw up at this point we are all scheduled to enter heaven bearing a close resemblance to the surrealist painter Salvador Dali in one of his most manic and apparently demonic moods. We fell on Thynn afterwards, of course, and the next night four of us sat around the carousel watching with eagle eyes and checking each slide as it went in with huge concentration. Each one is numbered, so in theory there is absolutely no reason why there should ever be a problem. When we did a little test run just to check that all was well, we discovered that the whole lot were in reverse order.

'Ah, but it doesn't matter, you see,' said Leonard excitedly, 'I'll just push the little button that says "back" when we want the slides to go forward, and then if we need to go back for any reason I'll just push the little button that says "forward", so if one gets stuck I'll just go forward one, but it'll actually be back, and then I'll go on going back so that we carry on forwards again. So we can leave them as they are.'

It being generally agreed that this had to qualify as one of the very worst and most deluded ideas in the entire history of terminally bad ideas, we took all the slides out again and replaced them the right way round. Once more four pairs of eyes studied the process closely. We *couldn't* have got it wrong. It was impossible for a mistake to have been made. We told each other that the thing was finally sorted. We promised each other that none of us would so much as breathe on the projector or the slides until it was time to show them.

That evening, despite our best and most concentrated efforts earlier on, a buzz of justifiable puzzlement ran through our audience as they learned that, contrary to popular belief, the Garden of Gethsemane is not in Israel at all, but is in fact located next to Boots, just off Lewisham High Street.

Those slides know. They are not inanimate. They know! I could swear that they sense when our concentration dips for a split second. When that happens they lick their little cardboard lips and flip gleefully around in the carousel, enjoying the thought of our discomfiture later on when at least two of them come out in the wrong order.

Don't like the way I get so ratty and intolerant with Leonard. It's almost as if, underneath all the things I think and say about everyone being equal in the sight of God, what I actually believe is that he's not as important as me, so it doesn't really matter what my attitude to him is, or how I speak to him sometimes. Wish I didn't keep tripping over these bits of myself that I've left lying around.

Later on I'll ask Gerald what he thinks. The only trouble is, being like his mother, he might tell me.

Wish these pathetic 'someone at the door needing a place to stay' jokes would come to an end. Before lunch Gerald came in and informed us that Brock and Brenda Badger were on the front-door step with Brian Badger, their adolescent son. Sighed heavily and buried my head in the paper, but Thynn had to ask, of course.

'What do Brock and Brenda Badger want?'

'Brock and Brenda Badger are very concerned about Brian Badger,' said Gerald. 'They're worried about his behaviour, and they're asking if he could move out of the forest and stay with us for a while so that he can sort himself out in a different sort of environment.'

'Why, what's he been doing?'

'Oh, typical teenager. Apparently he's been getting in with the wrong sett.'

The others fell about. Feel sorry for them.

Decided to spend the second half of my free day tackling one of these major shortcomings of mine. Announced during lunch that I would be doing some D.I.Y. until teatime. Foolish enough to hope for some warm support from the family.

Anne said, 'Oh, Adrian, is that really sensible? You surely don't actually enjoy spoiling bits of our house, do you? And if it's anything big or tricky we'll only have to get a man in to fix it all after you've finished making it worse. It's supposed to be my day off as well, you know.'

'Well, I – '

'I mean, let's face it, darling. You can't even mend a plug without having a minor nervous breakdown, can you? Remember the last time you did that? First of all you went ranting round the house like a homicidal lunatic because someone had taken your special little screwdriver with the blue handle from your second drawer down and forgotten to put it back. Then, of course, you found it in the third drawer down where you'd left it yourself after using it the time before. Then you found that it was no use anyway because you needed a Phillips screwdriver instead of an ordinary one, but you hadn't got one, so you went up to the shop but it was shut, and you came back and tried to get the screw out with a kitchen knife and got really savage, and said you wanted to strangle the plug and you ended up ruining the thread in the hole *and* the point of the kitchen knife and you had to throw both of them away and wait till the shop opened next day before you could buy a new plug.'

'Yes, but – '

'And when you got it back at last,' continued Gerald, 'you found that the new one needed a Phillips screwdriver as well and you still hadn't got one because you'd forgotten to buy one while you were up there for the second time getting the plug, so you had to go back a third time, and when you got back home I'd opened the plug and fixed it on in about a minute and a half with a thing on my penknife that isn't meant for that anyway, and you said what we holy ministers of the cloth would consider to be a very bad word and sulked for an hour. And that was just a plug.'

Said, with as much quiet dignity as I could muster, 'Well, thank you both for that. I feel really built up. Is there anything either of you would like to add to that resounding vote of confidence?'

'Dad,' said Gerald solemnly, 'you do have many fine qualities, but the truth will set you and us and our house free. You are to home maintenance what Mike Tyson is to synchronised swimming. Obviously when you were a little chap Grandpa never got round to explaining that the "D" in D.I.Y. doesn't stand for Damage, Devalue, Decimate or Destroy. And you do make some strange judgements. I vividly remember the day when you dug half the kitchen floor up to find a leak in the water pipe, and it turned out that the damp patch in the kitchen carpet was where my girlfriend Noreen's dog had piddled on the floor that morning.'

'I see. Anything you'd like to say, Leonard?'

Leonard likes being asked things. Steepled his fingers and tried to look wise.

'Okay, I've listened to Anne and Gerald.'

'Yes.'

'And there is something I'd like to say.'

'Ye-e-es.'

'Well, I've known you a number of years, Adrian.'

'Yes, I know that, don't I? Get on with it.'

'And I've been around a few times when you've set out to do something that you're not usually very good at.'

'Yesss!'

'And what I've noticed is that – okay, you do get things a little bit wrong sometimes – but the fact is that those times when you've really, really put your mind to the job in hand and tried as hard as you can – '

'Yes?'

'You've made a *complete* mess of it. I mean, a *wreck*. A disaster. A dismal, disappointing shambles of a – '

'Okay, okay, Leonard, that'll do, thank you very much. You've made your point. You don't have to stick it in and poke around with it as well. Right, well, despite what you've all said I still intend that this afternoon will be a milestone on the road to, er, on the road to – '

'Being able to fix a plug?' suggested Gerald helpfully.

'On the road to a new era of practical competence.'

They all made ridiculous pretending-to-be-impressed noises. Sounded like a trio of constipated owls.

I said, 'I've got that bird table kit in the garage that I bought two years ago. I intend to assemble it in the sitting-room this afternoon, and round about four o'clock we shall be able to watch the birds on it through the sitting-room window while we have our tea.'

Anne looked relieved. Gerald smiled that maddening smile of his, the one for which the Americans have an anatomically exact but unpleasantly vulgar expression that I couldn't possibly repeat here.

Thynn said, 'I don't mind eating outside, but how are you going to get the birds to come into the sitting-room?'

Understanding Thynn's mind is like learning to ride one of those bikes that go left when you steer right and right when you steer left. It can't be done without falling off and going mad yourself.

Left them all to wash-up while I fetched my bird table kit from the garage. Felt determined to prove everyone wrong. Told myself to be positive and assume that all those head-scratching, swearing, teeth-clenched, sweaty, wrong-tooled, having-to-take-it-apart-and-start-all-over-again experiences of the past were misleading.

Told myself, 'Face the future and be positive! You *can* assemble this bird table!'

Didn't feel that optimistic despite what I told myself. Felt sure my 'kit' was going to be like most other kits that I have ever had anything to do with. I was right, of course. If you look in a dictionary as I did before writing this, you will see that the word 'kit' is traditionally defined as 'a set of all the parts needed to assemble an item'. The people who were responsible for the alleged bird table that I've been wrestling with today must be free, post-modernist souls who scorn the idea of being tied down to such a tediously narrow definition. Or perhaps they use a different kind of dictionary altogether. If so, the relevant entry would read as follows:

Kit: noun. Random collection of parts bearing minimal relation to object or objects pictured on the side of the box in which they are bought. Usually accompanied by vast unwieldy sheet of instructions prepared by totally uncoordinated and spatially confused victim of a recent nasty head injury. Comes with polythene bag of randomly selected screws and strange, unidentifiable plastic things originally intended for the assembly of something quite different that happened to be within arm's reach of the person on Work Experience when the box was packed at the factory.

My son came in, still with that triangular grin on his face, as I was pulling the first, dumbly mysterious lumps of wood from the container. He pointed to one of the two claims that were printed boldly in capital letters on the side of the box.

ALL KINDS OF WILD BIRDS WILL BE
ATTRACTED TO YOUR TABLE!

Gerald said, 'Wow! Look at this, Dad! All kinds of birds. Pelicans, albatrosses – all kinds. Awesome! Just think of the

excitement that must be building up among all kinds of wild birds as the news gets round that an exceptionally attractive table is being assembled for their use at this very moment. Hey, I hope our garden's big enough, Dad. I mean, apart from all the thousands of normal little birds like sparrows and chaffinches and things there'll be flamingos here any minute from the zoo down the road, peering through the window to see how things are going. Then I suppose kites, eagles, vultures and South American condors will take a little longer to arrive. All the big flightless birds, ostriches, emus – that sort of thing – they'll have to be a bit more ingenious with their travel arrangements, but they're bound to turn up in the end, aren't they? Just picture it, Dad! Golden pheasants sitting side by side with peacocks and birds of paradise on our garden fence just waiting for you to emerge through the French windows with this wonderful new table. I tell you what – it'll make the set of that Alfred Hitchcock film *The Birds* look like an ornithological desert! If I was you, I'd – '

At this point I began to weary of Gerald's rather heavy-handed satire. Suggested he go and exercise his sparkling wit on his mother for a change. Got on with the job.

Halfway through, when I was in the middle of discovering that shapeless strut 'A' and alien base support 'F' must have been made in a completely different universe from each other and all the other pieces, I noticed the second claim on the side of the box.

EASY TO ASSEMBLE – EVEN A CHILD COULD DO IT!

Well, all right, yes, I expect one of those appallingly precocious children with the high-pitched, battery-operated voices who love to tell grown-ups they're doing things wrong could have easily assembled the contents of that infernal box, but I'd never allow a kid like that anywhere near anything I couldn't do.

Did assemble the bird table eventually. Bit of an exaggeration. What I actually did was to take the pieces of wood out of the box and screw them together in such a way that the result looked marginally more like a bird table than it used to look like some pieces of wood in a box. I suppose I did at least manage to fasten every bit of the theoretical bird table on to some other bit of the theoretical bird table, but when I'd finished and I stood back to view what I'd done, the result was inescapably theoretical, and it was hard to see how such an object could possibly be attractive to even one sort of wild bird.

Dragged my misshapen creation out through the French windows. Felt like some Doctor Frankenstein of the bird table world. Placed breadcrumbs and scraps of bacon on a tiny lumpy area in the middle that should have been large, flat and at the top, then retreated into the sitting-room just as the others brought tea in on trays. Anne closed the curtains and, after a few minutes, we peered out through the cracks. Gerald said, he didn't know why, but it made him feel depressed just to look at my bird table. Thynn asked why I'd smashed it up when he'd understood that I was planning to assemble it. Anne just shook her head despairingly.

Outside, an eerie hush seemed to have settled over the entire garden. It was the hush you imagine might fall after the explosion of a nuclear bomb, or in one of those deserted cowboy towns where tumbleweed is blown desolately along the street. After two or three minutes one small, retarded-looking sparrow flapped gormlessly into the area, then screeched to a

147

halt and reversed in mid-air as it spotted the grotesque, mutant form that crouched wretchedly in the centre of our lawn. Other than this, all kinds of birds were conspicuous by their absence.

My ex-kit, theoretical bird table is not a table by any definition, nor is it a resource for birds. It is a failure.

Said to Anne, 'I don't seem to have got very far with overcoming this particular shortcoming, do I?'

Anne said, 'Never mind, darling, don't be discouraged. No need to give up. Lots more to choose from.'

Asked Gerald after tea if he thought my attitude to Leonard was all wrong.

He said, 'Hmm, do you really want to know what I think?'

'Yes, 'course I do.'

'All right, well, it's no more all wrong than your attitude to mum and me is all wrong, Dad. The thing is he's become a part of our family really, hasn't he? And, whether it's right or wrong, I suppose families always have got the worst and the best of each other. You and he are a bit like brothers. You love each other and sometimes you really annoy each other, but nothing ever comes close to breaking the thing – the bond that joins you together. Ask yourself this, for instance. If and when Leonard and Angels get hitched – and my money's on that happening at some point in the future – who do you think Leonard's going to ask to be his best man? And now that his old mum's dead and gone, what family has he got except you and mum, and me when I'm around. I wouldn't worry too much, Dad. Leonard's a one-off and you've been given him to love and look after. Just do your best and let God look after the rest. That's my advice.'

'Thank you, Gerald,' I said, and I meant it.

Not often you see Gerald looking uncomfortable. A joy and a privilege to watch when it does happen, I must say.

Happened this time because he came along with me this evening to a church meeting led by George Farmer. Didn't really want to go, but the thought of George's forgiving expression when I saw him next was just too much to bear. George is a dear fellow, but he does seem to be stuck in one particular mode of delivery when it comes to doing Christian things up at the front. Began by making us get into groups of five or six. Gerald terrified everyone to death and caused a near stampede in our group by telling them he knew for a fact that George was planning to get us to describe our commonest sexual fantasies to each other.

In fact George said that we had to tell each other fifteen wonderful things that God had given us or done for us that day. Why does it always happen to me? All the groups around us seemed to have loads of things to thank God for. Really animated and leaning in towards each other tapping their hands with their fingers! My group sat miserably trying to think of just one. Eventually, Howard Blair said that he wasn't sure if it counted, but he'd quite enjoyed his lunch. Rest of us immensely relieved to at least have someone opening the score for our team. All nodded solemnly and meditated deeply on God's goodness to Howard in the matter of his lunch. Leonard then commented that he had quite enjoyed his breakfast, but that if we were talking about God having supplied it, perhaps we could pray that in future the bacon could be a bit leaner and the tomatoes a bit less runny. It was all snacks, meals and drinks after that. Couldn't seem to get off the subject.

George asked for feedback, and I'm afraid that's exactly what he got from us. All the other groups talked about 'special moments of intimacy with the Lord' and 'evidence of the Holy Spirit working powerfully in the lives of unbelievers'. The very best we had to offer was Howard's apple crumble.

Next, George said, 'Right, I'm going to ask you all a question.'

What George means when he says this is that he's going to *tell* us something, but that we're all going to have an immense amount of jolly fun guessing what it is first. I am truly fond of George, but when I see that playful light come into his eyes and I notice that his lower lip is spending an inordinate amount of time between his teeth, I can feel my jaw locking and my hands spontaneously curling into strangling shapes.

'Right,' said George with hideous joviality, 'here comes the question. Okay?'

He was building up the atmosphere.

'Okay, who is it in the Bible – who do we *know* in the Bible who really understood *inner wholeness*? Who really, really knew what inner wholeness was all about? And here's a little clue, folks. His name begins with a "J".'

Tricky one, eh? The fact was that, even without that subtle little clue, it would have been impossible to avoid being aware that the answer to the question was Jesus. The very tone of

George's voice signalled that fact without any doubt whatsoever. It was just a matter of who supplied the answer first.

'Oh, yes,' called out Gerald's voice unexpectedly from
beside me, 'I know the answer to that. It's Joseph, the one with
the coloured coat.'

George was paralysed for a moment, staring fixedly at
Gerald as if the world had suddenly started to spin the wrong
way, and he just wasn't able to work out how it could have
happened.

'Joseph,' he said in a flat voice. 'You think it was Joseph.'

All eyes turned to my son, and at the same moment I
realised that, unusually for him, Gerald was wishing he had
kept his mouth shut. He shielded his eyes with his hand and
mumbled a reply.

'Er, no, no, I didn't mean to say that – sorry. It wasn't
Joseph. It was Jesus. I meant to say Jesus. Of course it's Jesus.'

George wasn't going to let it go, though. When he next
spoke he sounded like one of those teachers who has caught
you talking to your neighbour and insists on having the contents of the conversation made public.

'No, Gerald,' he said, throwing his arms wide, 'I'm sure
we'd all like to know. We'd all like to know why you think it
was Joseph. If you could just share it with the rest of us we'd be
very grateful.'

'Well,' said Gerald, turning slightly pink, 'Joseph was, er –
he was thrown into a pit by his brothers, and while he was at
the bottom of the pit he really understood, er – '

There was no escape for him. The whole gathering was
hanging on his every word.

'While he was down at the bottom of the pit he must have really, really understood in-a-hole-ness.'

Comprehension passed through the assembly like a Mexican wave. Mostly groans and laughter with a few tuts of disapproval. George looked like I used to feel at school whenever I was faced with a quadratic equation.

When the noise had subsided he said, 'Right, Joseph was one, but the other was . . . ?'

Asked Gerald on the way home how he felt about what had happened at the meeting. Said he felt a bit fed-up because he'd recently decided to make a real effort to curb his flippancy when it wasn't going to be very helpful.

'It's like some kind of illness, Dad,' he said. 'I'm diseased with flippancy. It's terrible. Someone says something and I suddenly feel a funny thought tickling my stomach and then rising up my body until it comes out of my mouth. I just can't resist it sometimes.'

Asked him if he knew where it had all started.

He said, 'Well, for a start there's living in the same house as you for all these years, Dad.'

Couldn't work out whether that was a compliment or not.

'But apart from that, I think I know the exact moment when it began. It was when I was at school and I used to sit on the back row next to a boy called Smith. I only told mum about this at the time because I got into trouble for it afterwards and you wouldn't have understood. We were having maths one day with a teacher we all called "Glob" because he smoked this horrible stinking pipe in between lessons, and when he said things like "Appolonius' Theorem" he always sounded as if was trying to bring phlegm up from his throat so that he could spit.

Anyway, Smith brought some penny chews in one day. He or I quite often took food into the lessons, and we'd become top experts at chewing without actually moving our jaws, so – '

'Hmm, I'm *so* glad that your schooling wasn't entirely wasted.'

'Quite! So, anyway, we were sitting at the back as usual chewing these sweets and we must have been a bit careless, because old Glob stopped in mid-rumble, pointed in the general direction of Smith and I, and boomed out, "Are you eating, Smith?"'

'And I shouted back, "No, sir, I never touched him!" And everybody laughed and I got extra work to do.'

Said something after supper tonight that I thought was hilarious. I had gone out to the kitchen at Anne's request to see if something she'd put in the fridge for us was ready. It was a collection of little tubes containing some kind of fruit flavoured liquid that had to be left in the coldest part of the fridge until they were hard enough to be eaten like lollipops. Was inspired by the fact that, when I looked, some were ready and some were not. Spent a moment checking the reference in a Bible we keep in the kitchen. Really looked forward to being the one who told the joke for once.

When I went back in Anne said, 'Well, are they ready?'

I said, 'Matthew, chapter twenty-two, verse fourteen.'

'What does that mean?' said Gerald.

'Many are cooled, but few are frozen.'

Anne and Gerald looked at me as if I was someone who had appeared to be fairly sick, but was now revealed as being much more gravely ill than had been suspected.

Why is it always so much funnier when it's Gerald that says it?

TUESDAY, 25 SEPTEMBER

Despite great changes for the better in my son, the rumour that he has succeeded in growing up remains exactly that – a rumour. Walked up to the shop on the corner with him early this morning to get some stuff for making a few sandwiches for our journey. When I asked the girl behind the counter if she had any margarine, she said she had, and asked if there was any special brand we were looking for, because folks are getting more and more particular. Opened my mouth to reply but was interrupted by Gerald before I had a chance to get a word out.

He said, 'Well, actually there is one we'd prefer if you've got it. As far as I can remember, it's called: "Good heavens above! Are you telling me this isn't butter! You really do amaze me! Fan me with a crisp bread if this isn't the most butter-like margarine I have ever, ever seen! If you'd asked me to say what I thought this was I would have had no option but to say that it's the best, smoothest, creamiest and most unadulterated butter that it has ever been my pleasure and privilege to encounter. I am truly amazed!"

'That's what it's called.'

'We haven't got any of that,' said the girl, 'it must be new.'

Determined to find out how my book is doing. Rang Harry Waits-Round while we were filling up with petrol today. Picked his phone up after the fifth ring and said, 'What! Well, what! For God's sake, what!'

I said, 'It's Adrian here, Harry. How are you?'

He must love me ringing or visiting. It transfigures him. It transfigured him this time. He said, 'Adrian! Hey! Wonderful to hear from you! Made my day! Cheers for ringing, mate.'

Wished I truly believed I was the sort of person that my effect on him seems to suggest I am.

I said, 'Harry, we never quite got round to finishing our talk about how my book's doing.'

'You speak of the book that is making us all proud,' said Harry with impressive solemnity.

'Er, well, I hope so – the thing is, you didn't actually tell me how many copies have actually been sold – actually.'

Harry became very stern.

'I dare anyone to even suggest that we shall fail to sell out the entire print-run. I am personally committed to that, Adrian, and I say these words to you not only as a friend but also as a publisher.'

'How many has it sold so far?'

'A very shrewd question. Exactly!'

'What! Exactly what? How many has it sold?'

Heard a crackling noise that sounded a bit like a sheet of paper being screwed up, then Harry's muffled voice saying, 'Breaking up a bit at this end, Adrian . . . speak to you later . . .'

Bit disappointing to be cut off just as I was about to hear actual numbers at last. Think I might pop into the next Christian bookshop we come to and see how they're displaying my book and ask what the sales are like. That'll be encouraging.

In the van today got into a ridiculous discussion that almost turned into an argument with my stubborn son. Gerald may be very sharp and quick-witted and all that, but there are moments when he seems unaccountably dense. I recall the time, for instance, when the price of petrol had gone up, and I explained that the increase wasn't going to affect me because, in those days, instead of buying it by the gallon, I only ever bought five pounds worth of petrol at a time. His inability to grasp this simple fact seemed to drive him almost to the edge of hysteria.

Perhaps it's particularly bad with petrol, for some reason. I had just as much trouble getting through when I told him that I'd started using the next but one garage instead of the nearest one. I pointed out that I could get forty pounds worth of petrol into my car at the new one, but only thirty-seven pounds worth at the one just up the road. He simply *could not* comprehend what I was talking about. Strange, for one so bright.

Today's conflict was over the arrangement of groups for a sort of retreat day that I've been asked to lead in a few weeks' time. As Gerald quite rightly says, the church continues to force itself miserably into small groups on occasions like these, presumably because they think God wouldn't guess that anything religious was going on unless they did. Our argument was about the numbers in each group. Forty people are down to come to this event, and after trying to decide whether to have eight groups of five, five groups of eight, ten groups of four or four groups of ten, I had made a definite decision that it would be either eight groups of five or five groups of eight. At one point in the day each person present will be asked to talk for exactly one minute to the others in his or her group about their main reason for coming to faith.

Gerald said, 'Well, obviously it would be better to have eight groups of five from the point of view of time, wouldn't it?'

Stared at him.

I said, 'Gerald, how can the size of the groups possibly affect the time it takes? There are forty people there and if each one has to speak for one minute, it doesn't matter how you arrange the groups. There's always going to be one person speaking and the others in the group listening.'

He held his head in his hands for a moment, then said, 'Dad, you have to take the total amount of time that your forty people spend talking, and divide it by the number of groups in which each person is talking, and, assuming they all start and end at exactly the same moment, that will be the time it will take for everybody to complete their testimony. What you're talking about is a decision between the speaking lasting for five minutes or eight minutes.'

'No,' I said, shaking my head in disbelief, 'you haven't been listening, Gerald. They have to speak for one minute each, not five minutes or eight minutes. That would take far too long.'

'I *know* that!' said Gerald, raising his voice, perhaps because he knew he'd got a bit confused. 'What I'm saying is that all forty people will be finished in either five minutes or eight minutes depending on the size of the groups.'

Didn't want to be too hard on him. Said, as patiently and slowly as I could, 'Gerald, how can forty people, all speaking for one minute, one at a time, take five minutes to get through forty minutes of speech? Eh? Think about it.'

'But, Dad,' almost shouted Gerald, 'there'll be more than one person talking at the same time, won't there?'

'Well, no, there won't, because the rest of the people in each group have to listen to the person whose turn it is to talk. There'd be no point in that person talking otherwise, would there?'

Gerald looked as if he was going to say something else, then, after taking one or two deep breaths, clenched his teeth, turned and just drove on without saying anything else.

Not such a bad thing for him to learn that he can't always be right.

Went off to find the local Christian bookshop when we stopped for coffee this morning. Found it eventually in a small turning off the High Street. Odd name. It was called 'Fruit of the Grape'. Entered the shop trying to look as casual as possible but secretly hoping that staff and customers might recognise me and be really thrilled to meet me in the flesh. Walked around for a bit, but not a flicker. Forced eventually to introduce myself to the manageress, Mrs Harbin, a small, neat lady whose fixed expression was a disconcerting combination of vagueness and encouragement. She seemed moderately pleased to see me. Decided to ask her about the name of her shop.

I said, 'I was just wondering – I mean, a grape *is* a fruit, isn't it? How can the grape be the fruit of itself? Do you see what I'm getting at?'

Mrs Harbin said, 'The name was given to my husband during a time of prayer. I wanted to call it "The Ready Tongue", as in the psalm, but when Derek told me about "Fruit of the Grape", well, that was it. God's way is always best, isn't it?'

Thought privately that if God's way managed to avoid calling a shop 'The Ready Tongue' then it was certainly best.

'So, what actually is the fruit of the grape?'

'Well, it's a Christian bookshop.'

'Sorry, yes, I know. What I meant was, what actually *is* the fruit of the grape?'

'What is the fruit that you actually get from the grape?'

'Yes, what is that fruit?'

'What *is* the fruit?'

'Yes.'

'Well – it comes from the grape.'

'Yes, but what is it?'

'You mean what actually is the fruit?'

'Yes.'

'Well, it's – I'm not sure really.'

'Perhaps it's the wine, is it?'

Mrs Harbin clutched at this suggestion like a drowning woman grabbing at a lifebelt.

'Yes, yes, that'll be it. It's the wine. The fruit of the grape is the wine.' A sudden random inspiration. 'It's the wine of the Kingdom!'

'Ah, the wine of the Kingdom. And what precisely is the wine of the Kingdom?'

Long pause.

'Well – my husband would know.'

Gave up.

I said, 'What I really came in for was to ask how my new book's doing.'

'Your last book did really, really well!' said Mrs Harbin, suddenly animated. 'We sold lots of them.'

'Yes – excellent, thank you. And, er, how is the new one doing?'

'Well, there's been a tremendous lot of interest – you know, a lot of people pick it up and look at it for quite a few moments.'

'Pick it up and buy it, you mean?'

'Well, it's sort of building towards that over the weeks. I very nearly sold it on Wednesday. I'm sure it will go soon, and then my husband and I will have to sit down and decide whether or not to order another one.'

'It! One! Are you saying that you've only got one copy of my book?'

'Well, yes, we're only small, so we can't afford to take big risks.'

Bit depressed by the idea that ordering more than *one* of my paperback books might be seen as a wildly unpredictable financial investment. Hope this isn't a pattern for all the shops in the country. Must phone Harry Waits-Round again and find out.

Wish my son would put Barry out of his misery over this 'Jesus not telling the truth' thing. Barry leaned over to Gerald while we were having lunch today and spoke with a totally unconvincing air of confidence.

'Oh, I meant to say, I think I have finally solved your little puzzle, Gerald. You are obviously referring to the fact that there were times in the course of the Lord's ministry when it became necessary and appropriate for him to employ metaphor. It might reasonably be suggested that utterances employing such a figure of speech are not, in the strict sense, statements of fact, although one hastens to add that they do, of course, embody a truth that transcends mere factual accuracy. In the fifteenth chapter of the gospel of Saint John, for instance, the Lord refers to himself as the "vine", although clearly we are not intended to ascribe vegetative attributes to the person of – '

'Still wrong!' said Gerald, smiling that smile of his. 'Nothing to do with metaphor and nothing to do with parables. He made this statement about another person and he made it in one particular verse. Virtually given it to you there!'

Barry obviously didn't think so. Very crestfallen. Anne says his brain's liable to burst if he thinks about it much more. Told Anne it would make me very tense to be regarded as an expert on anything.

She looked at me, smiled and said, 'I think that's an area you can afford to relax in, darling.'

Seems a shame that someone like Angels should have let her sense of humour be corrupted by Gerald, Anne and Thynn. This afternoon, when we were all settled in the hotel lounge, she whirled in trying to look very excited. Might be a great dancer but her humour is as bad as all the others.

'Oscar Wilde's at the door!' she said. 'He's looking for a place to stay, and he told me that it doesn't matter if it isn't a real room, he'd be quite happy to curl up in any little storage space. And having said that,' she added with a dramatic flourish, 'he produced one of his great sayings.'

'Which one would that be, then?' asked Anne.

'He said, "Dear lady, we are all in the hall-cupboard, but some of us are looking up at the stairs."'

I don't know how much longer I can stand it. . .

Nearly choked to death on a piece of lettuce when we were eating in the hotel's restaurant before leaving for the meeting this evening. Thynn's stupid fault. Serve him right if I'd died and he'd had to do the talk.

What happened was, Gerald had been talking about how his church is just gearing itself up to support work being done to solve all sorts of social and medical problems in Africa. When he'd finished there was a pause and then Thynn said, 'I had something wrong with me once and I was the first person in the world to have it.'

One thing for sure. Picking up one of these casual cues of Leonard's is not something to be entered into lightly. Give him half a chance and before you know it you're blindly trudging along behind him across some uncharted, alien territory of the mind with no idea how to get back to base camp. Decided it wasn't going to be me this time.

'What was wrong with you, Leonard?' asked Anne kindly.

Thynn said, 'I was suffering from Odes.'

Silence.

'Odes.'

'Yes, that's right, Odes.'

All stared at Thynn. Could see Anne was struggling to make sense of what he'd said. She spoke haltingly.

'You don't mean people were making you listen to poems when you didn't want to, do you?'

Had a sudden mental picture of the young Leonard Thynn huddled in a dark cupboard in his bedroom, having Shakespeare's love poetry quoted brutally at him until he screamed for mercy.

'Classic case of textual abuse . . . ,' murmured Gerald.

'No, Anne, it was nothing to do with poems. I had Odes. I was an Odes sufferer.'

'No, you see Odes *are* poems, Leonard,' explained Anne gently. 'An ode is a poem with fourteen lines, and, as far as I can remember, it has to rhyme in a special pattern.'

'Oh, well, I don't remember any of that, but I do remember that Professor Bishop said I was definitely suffering from Odes.'

'You're sure you didn't mistake something he said? He couldn't have said – something sounding like that but different?'

'No, it was Odes. I had Odes. In fact he said that I was the very first person in the whole world to have it.' Pause. 'And then a little bit later he said that I hadn't got it and I'd never had it in the first place.'

Sighed to myself. As I'd feared. No map. No guide. Just a row of lost souls trailing along behind Leonard in a maze that had neither centre nor exit. There are times when Thynn makes Corporal Jones of *Dad's Army* look like a model of conciseness and relevance.

'Just a minute – who was the Professor Bishop you're talking about, Leonard?' asked Gerald, 'I'm getting quite intrigued by all this.'

'He was in charge at a place where I worked,' said Leonard. 'You know mother was always trying to find me jobs? Well, not long before she died she found me this quite good job at a place behind the shopping complex where they did research into new kinds of, er, neuro-something-patterning or something like that. Professor Bishop was in charge and after I'd been there a week, just doing odd-jobs all round the place, he called me in on Friday afternoon and told me that I'd got Odes.'

'But, Leonard, what exactly *is* Odes? None of us has heard of it.'

Thynn's eyes lit up as he remembered something.

'I've got it in one of my notebooks upstairs, Anne, the one that mother gave me to write down all the things that I've had wrong with me. I'll only be a minute!'

He flew off excitedly and arrived panting back a couple of minutes later with a battered old spiral-backed reporter's notebook. On the cover, in capital letters, were written the words:

THINGS WRONG WITH L. THYNN, FROM 1984 UNTIL THIS BOOK GETS FILLED UP OR HE DIES . . .

After flicking furiously through the lined pages of the book for a moment, he said, 'Ah! Here it is: "Friday – Told today by

Prof. Bish. that am suffering from Odes. Oral Disengagement Evasion Syndrome. Am first person in world to have it. Feel quietly proud."'

'Ah,' said Anne, 'that explains it. Odes is an acronym.'

'Is it?' said Thynn, 'I don't think so. Professor Bishop never told me it was one of those. He definitely said it was something you suffer from.'

'It is. Being an acronym just means that the letters – oh, never mind all that for now, Leonard. I'll explain later. What did they say this Oral Disengagement thingy was all about?'

'Well, Professor Bishop told me that since I'd started on the Monday, he and some of the others had been watching me, and they'd noticed a – a set of behaviours that made them think there was something a bit wrong with me. He said they'd observed how when it came to leaving an office or a meeting-room after bringing the post or collecting a bin or something I didn't seem able to just stop a conversation and go. I had to go on thinking of reasons to keep talking all the way to the door and right up to when I went out and turned the corner and they couldn't see me any more. And he said that they'd compared notes and found that the same sort of thing was happening in the corridors. Every time I saw someone coming towards me I'd stop and stand against the wall and talk to them right up to when they got fed up and went off down the corridor and disappeared.

'And he said they'd noticed that when I heard someone coming up the corridor behind me I always turned round and started speaking to them and then walked backwards in front of them still talking until they branched off into another bit of corridor or turned into one of the rooms or something.

Professor Bishop said people were beginning to find it a bit annoying, but that he'd given it a lot of thought and was convinced I couldn't help it because it was to do with some obsessional something or other I can't remember, caused by me not being confident enough on a very deep level to believe that people would want to see me and talk to me again if I broke off from talking to them. Then he said he'd never seen anything quite like it before, and for now he was going to call it Odes, which stands for what I just read out, and, as far as he knew, I was the only one in the world to have it, and he was sure, if I trusted him and put myself into his hands, he could help me in time.'

All totally transfixed by Thynn's account.

At last Anne said, 'But you told us just now, Leonard, that in the end Professor Bishop said you hadn't got – Odes, and never had had it in the first place.'

Leonard frowned.

'Oh, yes, he got rather cross, actually. You see, when I came in the next week there was nothing the matter with me, and when they all realised that, I thought I ought to explain to Professor Bishop how I'd managed to get completely cured over the weekend. I didn't want to tell him because I'd enjoyed having Odes and knowing that no-one else had ever had it, but – well, we are supposed to tell the truth, aren't we?'

'Of course,' said Anne. 'So you told him – what?'

'Well, that mother had gone to bed sick on the morning of my first day at work.'

'And?'

'And she had to stay there until the next Saturday.'

'So?'

'So she couldn't help me with anything until then.'

'And?'

'And I can't sew.'

'And?'

'I only had one pair of trousers to wear to work.'

'And?'

'I split them right down the back on my first morning at work . . .'

At this point the afore-mentioned piece of lettuce attempted a commando raid on the inside of my larynx and came very close to ending my life.

Bearing in mind Leonard's extraordinary account I asked Gerald later which had been the worst of the holiday and weekend jobs that he'd done while he was at school and during his time as a student. Said he'd give it some thought.

We were all really looking forward to tonight's event. It was being organised by a man called Victor Bradley, who said in his letters and on the phone that he was confident of selling six hundred tickets for tonight's event, so he'd booked the theatre in the middle of town and was planning to take us all out to a smart restaurant afterwards. Even better when he phoned briefly just after tea to say that he would come and pick us up in his big people carrier from our Guest House and drive us to the venue. Told him it wasn't necessary, but he insisted. All agreed there was a sort of warm glow around the forthcoming evening. We couldn't wait!

Bradley himself turned out to be one of those small round balding men who remain indomitably optimistic in the face of the clearest possible evidence that disaster is inevitable. Laughed and joked as he shook our hands in the lobby of the Guest House, then ushered us out, saying, 'Ladies and gentlemen, your golden chariot awaits!'

Our golden chariot was something of a shock. The only vaguely golden thing about it was the state of the bodywork.

'I am come that you might have rust,' murmured Gerald, 'and have it abundantly.'

I suppose you could have described Victor Bradley's manky old van as a people carrier in the bare sense that it carried people – if, that is, you stuffed most of them and their boxes of books into the back and made them sit on piles of old rugs and coats. Don't know what that van usually carries, but whatever it is, it's something that goes off in the end. Tried not to mind too much. After all, the event was the thing that counted, and we were still looking forward to that.

As Gerald and Leonard hefted the pictures and the projector equipment and two big boxes of books into the back of the van, Bradley said, 'Wow! You really are well stocked up with the old books, aren't you? Half a library there. Ha-ha! Sure you need that many?'

'Well actually,' I said, 'with an evening like this it might not even be quite enough.'

'Oh, good heavens, yes, dead right!' he said. 'Who knows what might happen! We believe in miracles, don't we?'

Slightly puzzled by this comment.

Van coughed and spluttered and didn't seem to want to start at first, but we got going eventually. I sat at the front next to Bradley, who had to stir the long gear stick like a wooden spoon in a Christmas pudding mixture every time he changed up or down. Very noisy vehicle. Had to speak quite loudly over the noise of the engine.

'So, Victor,' I said, relishing the immanent buzz and excitement of the event that was to come, 'you didn't have too much trouble getting rid of your six hundred tickets, then?'

'Well,' he wrestled violently with the gear stick as we started up a slight incline, 'we didn't quite make the old six hundred, but in the end, well, the Lord will bring the ones he wants, won't he? Praise God!'

Tried to ignore a loud snort from Gerald in the back, audible even over the noise of the engine. I knew my son's views on the theory that the Lord brings the ones he wants. He reckons it usually means that the advertising has been useless, the project is unattractive and the locals are unlikely to take a chance on coming after the last disaster. Didn't want to discourage Victor, though, after all his hard work.

'Actually,' I said, 'from the point of view of talking to people and selling books and – well, achieving a feeling of intimacy, it's sometimes better to have slightly fewer people. So how far short of the six hundred were you in the end, or don't you know exactly?'

'Bearing in mind what you've just said, I'm quite relieved,' said Bradley, 'because we didn't actually make the five hundred either. So! Lots and lots of intimacy! Praise the Lord!'

'Never mind, four hundred odd is a good number. I think we'll all settle for that. That's more than we're expecting anywhere else, Victor, so well done.'

'Oh, I can promise you it'll be even more intimate than that!'

Bradley somehow managed to made it sound as if the news was getting better and better.

'More intimate than that? Three hundred?'

'I think we'll be a tad short of the three hundred mark,' he said, 'although you never know how many you're going to get on the door, do you?'

'A tad?'

'Well, let's put it like this, old man – if we're up to two hundred and fifty I shall be very pleased and surprised.'

'I see. Right. But, Victor, aren't two hundred people or more going to rattle around a bit in a theatre that holds six hundred?'

'You have hit the proverbial on the proverbial!' he exclaimed, as though I'd won *Mastermind* with my specialist subject: 'Whether or not you want two hundred and fifty people rattling around in a theatre that holds six hundred, and that's precisely why I made an executive decision to scale the operation down a bit. I cancelled the theatre, which was a pricey venue, and settled on a place that suited the numbers!'

His whole tone was of one who has prepared and executed an enormously complex plan with huge success. It was ridiculous. On the other hand, over two hundred still seemed pretty good.

'Right, so after all that, where are these two hundred odd people coming to hear us this evening?'

Bradley sucked air in between his teeth as though, in some way, I had rashly and vastly overreached myself.

'Topping the two hundred is a bit ambitious,' he said, 'and as you so rightly said, Bro, we can't have them rattling around in some huge space, can we?'

'Less than two hundred, then?'

'Really intimate!'

'More than a hundred?'

A roar from the engine and another grapple with the gear stick as we hit a second incline.

'Bit more intimate than that! Just under the ton I would think!'

Didn't dare ask any more after that. Our wild and wacky evening with six-hundred people cramming into a centrally located theatre had already shrunk to an audience of less than a hundred, presumably having to trail into some dismal church hall on the outskirts of the town. No wonder he'd thought we might have too many books. Sank into gloom then pulled myself together. After all, the eighty or ninety people who were gathering to hear us that evening were just as important in God's eyes as anyone else. Numbers were not everything. Began to cheer up a bit.

Eventually pulled up outside a semi-detached house in a fairly ordinary, leafy street. Victor pointed out of his window and said, 'Voilà! Chez Bradley! Time for a good old brew, eh?'

Let the others out of the back of the van. They looked crushed and bumped and fed-up, but the thought of tea cheered us all up. Victor showed us into a living-room, where there were seven or eight people – Victor's team, I assumed – sitting around the edge of the room. Victor's wife, Lola, small and round and apparently as pointlessly positive as her husband, brought us tea and biscuits, the first good thing that had

happened since we left the Guest House. All very nice, but after a while I glanced at my watch and realised it was getting late. Leaned over to show Bradley my watch.

'Er, Victor, time's pushing on. Shouldn't we be getting down to the venue to get set up and all that?'

He looked at me as if I'd lost my mind.

'This *is* the venue, Adrian, my friend! Perfect, don't you think? Just right, size-wise. Intimate and cosy.'

Could hardly speak.

'But what about the audience?'

'Why, they're here, old boy.' He gestured around the room with one hand. 'Eight of the best, all waiting to hear what you have to say to them. Did you want to get the books and the rest of the stuff in?'

It was like a slap in the face with a frozen haddock, but we had a choice. We could rant and rage, or just grin and bear it. Decided on the latter, probably for all the wrong reasons.

Didn't use the projector for obvious reasons. Brought in just a few books from the van. Asked Angels if she'd rather not dance in such a ludicrously tiny area, but to my surprise she said she'd go ahead. Partly, she said, because it reminded her a bit of the old people's home.

'Anyway,' she added in a whisper, squeezing my arm and smiling as she spoke, 'we're all in it together, aren't we? We'll just do it, shall we?'

Really loved her for that.

Funny how things work out, isn't it? There was something about that funny little evening we did for eight people in a front sitting-room in a house in a suburban street that was as special as any other part of the tour. They loved Angels and they seemed to enjoy listening to Gerald and I talking about why we thought we would go on following Jesus, however good or bad things were for us. Throughout it all, Victor, who'd screwed everything up about as thoroughly as it could be done, nodded and smiled proprietarily, as though this was the exact fulfilment of his original, extravagant dream.

The most amazing thing about the evening was what happened at the end of the meeting, when we had finished the formal part and one or two people were expressing interest in having a look at the books and pictures.

Angels suddenly stood up and said rather nervously, 'I, er, hope nobody minds if I just say something.'

Silence fell. She looked from face to face around the room.

'It's just that, well, I'm not a Christian like the rest of you – if you all are, I mean. But I've been listening to Adrian and Gerald and Anne and Leonard talking about Jesus since I met them, and I've decided that I want to follow him like they do. So, would anyone mind if I just kneel down here and give my life to him now, because – ' tears welled up in her eyes 'it's – it's not been a lot of use to me for a long time now.'

Strange, moving moment.

Leonard was in tears as well, and Anne and I weren't far off either. Even Barry seemed to be temporarily distracted from theory by such a vivid example of practice. Angels simply dropped to her knees and, for all that she may be capable of being needlessly obscure at times, it was the simplest prayer you can imagine. Anne said a prayer afterwards and gave her a hug, and then we had another cup of tea and one or two people bought books. One of the eight people even handed over a cheque in exchange for one of Zak's paintings.

Wasn't holding out much hope for the 'smart restaurant'. Assumed it would have been 'scaled down' just as the venue had been. I was right. It had turned into a plate of sandwiches and a slice of cake, offered to us by Victor and Lola as though these things constituted a feast that could not help but exceed our wildest expectations.

As we were loading up the 'golden chariot' in preparation for leaving, Gerald said quietly, 'Do you think Victor's scaled down the money, as well, Dad? He can't have made much from eight people buying tickets, can he?'

I thought that was a very good question.

Back at the Guest House, after the others had said their goodbyes and taken the stuff in, I shook hands with Victor and said, 'Victor, you did say that you'd be able to spare a couple of hundred pounds from ticket sales tonight, and we've budgeted for that. Our trip depends on it. Do you want to give me a cheque, or would it be just as easy for you to pop back with it in cash before we leave tomorrow morning?'

He never blinked an eyelid. Took a sealed envelope from his pocket and handed it to me.

'Adrian, mate,' he said, 'here is a complete tally of all income and outgoings together with a cheque drawn on my personal account for the agreed fee. It's been a pleasure, and I do hope we can do it again some time!'

As the golden chariot pulled away I felt a little guilty. All that money out of his personal account. It didn't seem fair, really.

My guilt only lasted up to the point when I opened the envelope and read what Victor had written on the piece of paper that I found inside.

income

Eight people at five pounds per person = £40

outgoings

Expenses : tea, cake, petrol etc. = £13

remaining disposable income = £27

40% to me, as agreed = £10 – 80p
60% to you, as agreed = £16 – 20p

As well as this sheet of paper there was a cheque drawn on Victor's account for the sum of sixteen pounds and twenty pence. Showed this to Barry, who, to his credit, didn't turn a hair.

'He promised you a percentage, Dad, didn't he?' said Gerald when I told him what had happened. 'The two hundred depended on him selling all those tickets. We'll have to pay for the hotel now – or Barry will. You must feel really mad. He can't have done *anything* at all.'

I shook my head and gestured with my hand towards Leonard and Angels sitting on a nearby sofa, their heads close together, deep in conversation.

'I don't actually mind that too much, Gerald,' I said. 'Somebody did something.'

Doing a meeting tomorrow lunchtime in the sitting-room of a house called 'The Willows' in a district known as Critchley Park. Gerald says he knows it and it's one of those ultra-posh areas where everyone's got three cars and huge gardens and the approach roads are deliberately not looked after all that well, in order to discourage the *hoi-polloi* from coming to stare at things they can never have. Said I thought he might be being a little unfair. He agreed, but said he'd bet me anything I liked that the meeting would be full of rich ladies with problems that can't be solved with money.

We shall see.

WEDNESDAY, 26 SEPTEMBER

Finally came to a realisation in the middle of the night that the time has come to follow that good old Christian precept – if you can't beat 'em, join 'em. In this case I was thinking of Gerald, Anne, Leonard and Angels with their ridiculous, time-wasting succession of jokes about homeless people coming to the door. Some dreadful examples over the last months have included:

Sir Galahad's servant seeking a bed for the knight.
A hippie called Lily looking for her own pad.
A test dummy wanting somewhere to crash.
An effeminate computer programmer who
    was happy to DOS down on a
    camp-bed.
A mime artist holding a girlie
    magazine and a toffee
    who was – wait for it –
    hoping for a
    penthouse
    suite.

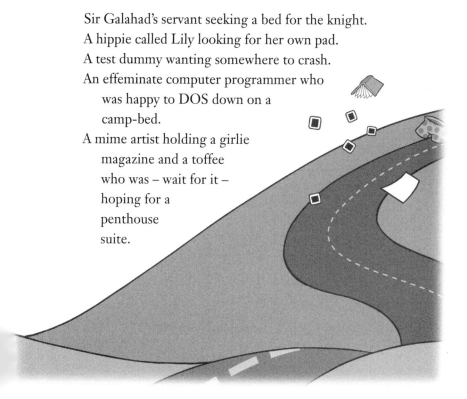

Have decided I'll play them at their own game. Spent ages in the small hours thinking up one of my own. Very keen that it should be cleverer and funnier than any of theirs. So pleased about what I came up with in the end that it was all I could do to keep from laughing out loud. Stuffed my knuckles in my mouth to avoid waking Anne up. Can't wait until later!

Gerald appeared this morning holding a piece of paper in his hand.

'Been thinking about what you asked yesterday afternoon, Dad – about jobs. I suppose the ones where I had to pretend I was busy were the worst. It was such hard work trying to look as if you were doing something. Much easier if you actually had something to do. The time passed really quickly. I mean, do you remember that job I got in a hotel down near Bourne-mouth for the summer? I've just been thinking that if the job had been advertised exactly as it turned out for most of the people like me who were working there, the ad. would have read something like this.'

He handed me the sheet of paper. I smoothed it out and read it.

> Idle, immature young man required for poorly organised and indefinable duties in seaside hotel. Must have ingenious and creative approach to time-wasting. Ability to hurry briskly around with absorbed, distracted expression on face an advantage.
>
> The person selected to join our team will demonstrate an adeptness at abruptly reversing direction as though recalling

urgent business requiring immediate attention in the place from which he has just briskly hurried. In addition he will be expected to carry vaguely important looking sheets of paper which he will read as he walks, scratching his head and clicking his tongue with impatience as though faced with the task of sorting out some other person's stupid mistake.

Our successful applicant will be spotted only rarely and always in the distance by those who are responsible for his work, but on each occasion he will appear far too involved in other obscure but crucial activities to be called away for the purpose of involving himself with such trivia as his normal duties.

Dalliance and inappropriate involvement with female members of staff of a similar age during working hours will be an important feature of this person's daily responsibilities, as will a brusque and off-hand manner to guests on those occasions when he is unable to avoid them.

Wages will be commensurate with a role that requires the bare minimum of actual work, but we would expect the applicant that we appoint to complain continually about rates of pay and, after the first three or four weeks in post, to develop and ferment opposition to management among other workers on the basis of pay and conditions.

Chronic lateness and absenteeism together with unconvincing excuses about visits to the dentist and deceased fantasy grandmothers are compulsory.

If you think this might be the post for you, ring Brian on Mudbanks 385924, lie about your previous experience, and ask for an application form, which should be filled out as though you were an illiterate Patagonian who has just consumed half a bottle of gin and is using a biro that has had the top left off it for a fortnight. We dread hearing from you.

'Good heavens, Gerald,' I said as I laid the paper down, 'was it really like that?'

'Well, I suppose that might be a bit of an exaggeration, but yes, by and large, and collecting together the experiences of most of the casual workers who were there, it was more or less like that.'

'Well, I don't remember you ever telling mum and me.'

He chuckled and patted my arm.

'Dad, if I'd been mean or brave enough to tell you and mum half the alarms and crises and near disasters that happened to me from when I was about seventeen right up until I finished college, you would hardly ever have slept. As it was, they got sorted somehow, they just passed, and you never needed to know.'

Quite stunned by hearing this. Couldn't decide whether I was glad to have escaped all that worry, or a bit upset that we'd been left out and not been able to help.

Thought very carefully about phoning Harry Waits-Round this morning before leaving for my lunchtime meeting. Decided the only way to get a straight answer about my book was to ask a direct question and not let him talk about anything else until he'd answered it. Dialled his number and after the sixth ring he answered.

'No! No! No! No! No! A billion times no! Whatever it is, the answer is still a big fat smelly no! And if you keep on ringing me I shall come down there and personally insert – '

'Harry, it's Adrian here, Adrian Plass.'

182

'Aaadrian!' I could almost hear the transformation. 'This is great! I thought you were someone from one of the other offices that I've been having a – you know, a bit of a joke with. Ha-ha! So, what can I do for you on this bright and happy morn, mate?'

I said, 'Harry, if you don't mind I'd like to ask you a very simple question. And when I've finished asking it, could you please, please not say anything at all except for giving me a very, very simple answer? Would you mind doing that?'

'No problemo! Just my style in fact. Ask on, Macbeth!'

Ignored the untrue statement and the pointless, completely inaccurate Shakespeare quotation.

'Right, please could you tell me simply and clearly how many copies of my book have been sold? Nothing else. Just a number.'

Silence for a few moments, except for the sound of Harry operating his keyboard, presumably bringing up the sales statistics.

'Right, I am very pleased to be able to tell you that, as of last Friday, your book had sold thirty-four thousand, five hundred and forty copies.'

Really amazed and delighted.

'Oh, I see! Well, that's great! I'm so pleased.'

'All part of the service, my old mate.'

'Well, thanks again, and I'll see you soon.'

'Any time! Always a pleasure. And let's hope the new book does just as well as time goes by, eh?'

Only dawned on me what he'd said as I heard his phone being put down. I *still* don't know how the new book is selling. Getting a bit fed-up with Harry. Beginning to think he doesn't want to tell me. If I wasn't a Christian I think insertion might be the way to go.

Interesting thing at the lunchtime meeting for the very posh ladies with deep problems that can't be solved with money.

Gerald was more or less right. The event was held in one of those big country house sitting-rooms where there's no clutter and absolutely everything is top of the range. Noticed three or four of those big, heavy table lamps that you see in the windows of shops in Cheltenham but can't imagine anyone actually buying when the money could be used to get groceries for a month. Most of the women seemed to be wearing the equivalent of the cost of a whole aisle at Sainsbury's as well. All immaculate.

Felt a little self-conscious as we sat down on discovering a small but virulently coloured egg stain on my jumper that I must have picked up at breakfast. Tried to surreptitiously wipe it off with some spit on the end of my finger, but it wouldn't budge. Then tried scraping it with my thumbnail. Worked too well. The hardened bit of egg took off from my jumper and flew away onto the Bible that was lying in the lap of the lady in the chair next to me. She was talking to the lady on her right and didn't notice. Tried to look as if nothing had happened and waited to see what she would do when she found that a lump of dried fried egg had miraculously appeared on her Bible. Watched, hypnotised, out of the corner of my eye as she turned eventually and registered the alien presence, calmly took a tissue from her sleeve and carefully wiped her nose, then scooped

the bit of egg up with her tissue and poked it back into her sleeve. True class!

There were mostly ladies there, but two or three men as well. It was in connection with one of these men that the interesting thing happened. He was sitting directly opposite me at the other side of the room on a straight-backed chair. He had one of those square, grizzled, heavy-eye-browed, rather bad-tempered faces, a bit like one of those old men who used to sit in the theatre box during *The Muppet Show* and criticise everything. He sat without moving from the moment I arrived, even before I started speaking, glaring directly into my face with a sort of furious amazement, as though his mind could barely credit the staggering depths of idiocy that my appearance suggested. Wondered with a slight flush if he'd noticed the egg incident.

Even worse when I did start my talk. The eyebrows drew closer and closer together, the mouth turned farther and farther down at the ends, and the eyes bulged with murderous disbelief as I began to talk about the power of love and the gentleness with which God heals broken hearts.

Found myself conjecturing that this crusty old devil had probably come along wanting to hear good common sense about setting the world to rights and getting tough with immigrants and clearing beggars off the streets rather than all this pathetic, namby-pamby drivel about love.

So off-putting! Did my best not to look at him too much as I went on, but I couldn't help it. My eyes kept getting dragged back to that little patch of human darkness directly in front of me. By the time I was a quarter of an hour into my forty-five minute talk I wasn't able to see anything else. In fact, his face seemed to swell and grow larger and larger until the whole room was filled with that one head and those bristling eyebrows and that grimly disapproving mouth.

Finished at last after about a year. Slight beading of sweat on my brow as I received a genteel patter of applause from the ladies and heard the usual perfectly timed clatter of china and cutlery approaching from the direction of the kitchen. Relieved to see that my critic's head had regained its normal size, but panicked suddenly as I realised that the man had risen from his chair and was making his way towards me. The face, fiercely irascible as ever, was moving across the room in my direction. Into my mind flashed the bit in *Jurassic Park* when the Tyrannosaurus Rex starts to approach. The *face* was coming to say something to me! It was going to chew up what I had said and spit it out. I was going to be told exactly what this man thought of the half-witted rubbish I had just been spouting. Almost got up and backed out of the door. Too late! The face was upon me. It was leaning towards me. A hand was placed upon my shoulder. Words were coming out of the bridge-shaped mouth.

'Just wanted to tell you how much your talk meant to me. Exactly what I needed this morning. Thanks a lot.'

Gulped something in return. It had been like finding Genghis Khan and his hordes on your doorstep, all with bunches of flowers concealed behind their backs. Realised yet again that you can never, never, ever judge by appearances – until the next time, of course.

Overheard a snatch of conversation in the van while I was driving this afternoon that goes a long way towards explaining why Leonard and Angels are so well suited.

After talking for a bit about how much they were enjoying the tour, Angels said, 'The thing is, Leonard, I've never really been very good at team things. I don't usually enjoy being part of a group.'

'Oh, well, join the club!' agreed Thynn with considerable warmth.

Muffled snort from Gerald.

'Actually, that's a good idea,' said Angels. 'We could start a club for people like us who don't like joining things.'

'Yes,' agreed Leonard, 'and we could have a rule that when we meet we don't have to join in if we don't want to, and if anyone breaks the rule he won't be allowed to be part of the club any more.'

'Well, I'd join a club like that,' said Angels.

'So would I!' said Thynn.

'I think lots of people would.'

'So do I.'

'People who don't like joining clubs.'

'Right!'

'Well, let's start it.'

'All right, let's.'

'What shall we call ourselves?'

Thoughtful silence.

'I know!' said Thynn. 'What about calling ourselves the Not Everyone Enjoys Joining In Things Society?'

'Yes, Leonard, I like it. It has a sort of ring to it.'

'We'll be known as the NEEJITS.'

'Yes,' muttered Gerald sleepily from his corner, 'I think you probably will.'

Somehow think Leonard and Angels will be very happy together.

When we were all crowded together again just before teatime in the twin room that Anne and I have got, I slipped out, banged on the door, then came back into the bedroom. As I came in Anne was saying, 'And in the early hours of the morning I woke up and he seemed to be trying to eat his own hand. Sometimes I really do get – oh, hello, darling, who was that knocking on the door?'

Felt so indignant that I forgot all about my joke for a moment.

I said, 'Excuse me, Anne, but I was not eating my own hand. I was stopping myself from laughing so as not to wake you up. I thought you were asleep. If I'd known you were awake obviously I would have just laughed out loud. You know, if people sometimes just took the trouble to find out – '

'So you weren't eating your hand,' said Thynn, 'you were just stuffing it in your mouth to prevent yourself from laughing hysterically in bed in the early hours of the morning, right? Well, I must say that sounds perfectly normal to me.'

He looked enquiringly at the others.

'Do it all the time,' said Gerald.

Angels said, 'Me too – not.'

'Anyway, darling, never mind that now. Who was at the door?'

Suddenly remembered. Felt good to be the one in control for once. Left a little pause before answering.

'It was a chicken.'

Anne said, 'A chicken? At the door?'

'Yes – well, a hen.'

'A female chicken.'

'Yes, that's right.'

'A hen rung the front door bell?'

'Yes, it did.'

'How?'

'Er – it was one of those hens that can flutter up to a certain height.'

Thynn produced a vastly overacted sigh. Said, like some world-weary therapist, 'I very much fear that we're off into the world of eating our own hands again.'

'No-o-o we're not,' said Gerald, with one of those infuriating American grins plastered all over his face. 'I've just clicked. I know what's happening. Dad's having a go at one of our jokes, aren't you, Dad? Come on, admit it! You are, aren't you? You are!'

Shrugged and replied, 'All I'm saying is that there was a hen at the door.'

They all looked at me as if I was a frog who'd proposed to Britney Spears.'

'So, presumably,' said Angels, 'this hen has a bit of an accommodation problem, eh?'

'Well, yes, she does. And er, she's a very unusual hen.'

Pause.

'What sort of unusual hen?' asked Anne. 'This is beginning to sound quite interesting.'

'Well, she's a contortionist hen. In fact, she's probably better at being a contortionist than any other hen in the world. She was probably the Olympic gold medal-winning contortionist hen of the last, er – chicken Olympics.'

Really had their attention by now.

'Right, so let's just take a look at this,' said Gerald slowly. 'What we have here, according to dad, is a homeless chicken who is better at being a contortionist than any other hen in the world. And she rings our bell and says that she's looking for – what?'

Time for my grand punch line.

'Well, she's, er, looking for somewhere to lay her head. *Lay* her *head*, you see. She's a contortionist hen, so . . . '

Total, stricken silence. Hardly the wildly ribald response I'd anticipated.

Gerald said quietly and seriously, 'Dad, that is *gross*. That is not funny, it is gross.'

'Unpleasant – particularly, if I may say so, for women,' said Angels.

'That's not what you were laughing about in bed, was it?' asked Anne a little worriedly.

'An insult to chickens, and indeed to fowl of all varieties, everywhere,' said Thynn foolishly.

Atmosphere so frozen that, after a moment or two, I decided to just slip out of the door and go down to the hotel sitting-room to look for people who hadn't heard my gross, anti-female, insulting chicken joke and wouldn't judge me accordingly. As I shut the bedroom door behind me there was a loud chorus of laughter from inside the room, and I heard Gerald's voice shouting out, 'Hold on, Dad – wait for us! Last one downstairs is a chicken!'

Forgave them after Gerald bought me a toasted teacake, Anne ordered tea all round, Angels suddenly cackled over the idea of a chicken laying its own head, and Thynn admitted that he hadn't understood what I was talking about anyway.

It's all very funny, I suppose, but they're supposed to be keeping my feet on the ground, not burying them in concrete.

At least the 'someone at the door' jokes will stop now – won't they?

Barry's entire life seems to be revolving around Gerald's claim that Jesus said something that wasn't true. On the way to the meeting tonight, reading his Bible by torchlight in the back of the van, he once again announced that he had solved the puzzle. Thought I detected a rather feverish tone in his voice.

'You postulated a verse that makes mention of a particular person,' he said, 'and I am convinced that you are referring to the thirty-third verse of the eighth chapter of the gospel according to Saint Mark, where the Lord addresses Simon Peter as "Satan". In doing so he was not, of course, suggesting that Peter was in fact the embodiment of the devil, but that he – '

'Wrong!'

'Well, in that case there is that verse in which the Lord, in his suffering on our behalf, cries out that he has been forsaken by his father, whereas – '

'Wrong!'

No more from the back of the van after that except for heavy breathing and the sound of thin pages being flipped over one by one.

Bizarre episode before the meeting started this evening.

Felt a bit nervy just before the off, so I went outside and walked up and down the gravel path by the entrance doors for a while. Found myself wishing it was possible to be a non-smoker who smokes from time to time. Something about the muted buzz of expectation from inside the building that made me feel quite frightened. All those people waiting for me. They were waiting for *me*! They'd paid real money to listen to *me*! If I didn't turn up nothing would happen. Who on earth did they think I was? Who on earth did *I* think I was?

Fantasised about climbing over the fence in the distance at the back of the car-park and running through a thick belt of trees to the main road, and then finding a taxi or a bus or something to the nearest railway station. I could just disappear for ever, and get a flat up north and have big fried breakfasts and work at the supermarket and go to the cinema and drink too much sometimes, and stop worrying about my silly faith and I would never have to go back into that hall and face those rows of people who had probably only turned up to disapprove of me and dislike me and make me feel as if I never was a proper Christian anyway.

My family and friends would miss me, of course, I reflected, but as time gently poured its balm of healing on the wounds of their hearts I would become a special, sweet, sad, lingering memory that they carried carefully with them like a pitcher of spring-water to their graves. Almost wept at the thought of their grief and unhappiness. Pictured articles in the Christian press speculating as to reasons for my strange disappearance. Kidnapped by Satanists? Abducted by an atheistic foreign power? Whisked away by the Spirit like Philip in the New Testament, to do essential work for God in some far country? Perhaps an article in one of the loonier magazines would suggest that the rapture had happened and I was the only one who had been found worthy.

Interrupted at this intelligent point in my musings by glancing at my watch and realising that the meeting was about to begin. Apologised for my thoughts to God, who probably hadn't been listening anyway, and went back inside. Always do in the end.

Sat on a bench against the back wall while proceedings opened with a few minutes of communal singing. Just after the first song started the organiser hurried over, sat on the seat beside me and put his mouth next to my ear.

He said, 'Sorry, I know you're bound to be a bit distracted at the moment, but I wonder if I could ask you to do us a small favour?'

'Yes, yes, of course. You've only to ask.'

Always respond like that when I'm in Christian speaker mode.

'Well, one of our very keen helpers, Mrs Belper, a lady you have not yet met, tells me that she spotted a man outside just now who looks as if he's trying to make a decision about whether to come in or not. Very troubled. A soul in torment. That's how she described him. Mrs Belper didn't want to approach him herself because, er, she's a woman, and she is a little – but still, I just wondered if you might have popped out quickly and said an encouraging word or two to – you know – to encourage him.'

Agreed to go, then spent two absurd minutes hunting for Mrs Belper's soul in torment before realising that I was earnestly searching for myself. Very successful in persuading myself to come in for a second time. Can't help feeling that Mrs Belper must have been impressed and astonished to see that the deeply troubled someone who nearly didn't come in at all had been so transformed by a minute or two of counselling, that he was now the speaker for the evening!

Funny thing. Nearly always, as soon as I actually start speaking, the worries all disappear. Talked tonight about how God says he'll write his law in our hearts, but how difficult it can be when the devil has made sure that graffiti gets sprayed over our hearts when we're little, and there's not much space left.

Great evening in the end. Angels danced her heart out in the 'tiny' space allocated to her, and only two of the slides were in the wrong place. Amazing!

Right at the end, when everyone except a few of the helpers had gone, Gerald beckoned me to the back of the hall where a man was sitting all on his own on a chair by the door.

'This is Simon, Dad,' said Gerald softly. 'He wants to tell us about a bit of graffiti.'

Gerald takes the mickey out of me all the time, but when he does warm, cooperative, him-and-me things like this it nearly brings tears to my eyes. Made a little triangle of three chairs and sat down.

Simon was in his early fifties, dressed in jeans, check-shirt and a short coat made of heavy cloth. He was clean-shaven, trim and competent looking, with tight greying curls, kind eyes and a determined chin. When he spoke, though, his voice was heavy with pain.

He said, 'Don't want to waste your time. It's just a silly thing. You're going to think it's really small and silly, but it hurts so much. It's always hurt a bit. Tonight, though – I dunno – it's like there's a sort of throbbing ache in my heart. Can't stand it!'

He bowed his head over his folded arms. Assumed it must be something to do with childhood neglect or abuse. Sighed inside as usual. What on earth was I going to say to this man?

'As little as possible would be a reasonable option,' replied a little voice in my head.

'What's it about, Simon?' asked Gerald.

Long pause, then Simon lifted his head and said, 'It's about homework.'

'R-Right.'

Tried to nod as gravely as if he'd said it was ritual abuse or murder. He lifted an arm to gesture in my direction.

'You were talking about what happens when we're little. Well, I'm not talking about when I was very young, although there were – you know – other things then, things that weren't so specifically about me. I was about thirteen when this happened. At Grammar School. I passed the eleven-plus. Big deal then, I can tell you. I was good at English, probably because I'd always read lots of stuff, but the whole school thing was just chaos really. For me, I mean. I didn't want it to be, you understand. What I wanted – what I *wanted* more than anything in the world was to be one of those organised types who always had their pencils and pens in a nice case, and a bottle of blue-black ink that the top hadn't worked loose on, and every single one of the books we were supposed to bring to each of the classes with us, all in a sensible bag that hadn't got lost on our third day at school. I *wanted* to do my homework on time and have it marked and find out what the teacher wrote underneath it in red, and be proud of my marks when they were good, and – and make progress.'

Simon shook his head slowly from side to side and stayed silent for a moment.

After a while I cleared my throat and said, 'So, what stopped you being like that, like the ones who got everything right?'

He stared at me.

'It's funny, isn't it? When you're a kid you sort of automatically take all the responsibility on yourself, don't you? It just doesn't seem to click that the limited little universe you've grown up in and the way others treat you might have something to do with the way you are – the way you behave and manage in the rest of the world. I mean, I can't remember ever saying to myself that, given the state of my family and my home and the – the emotional glue I had to drag myself out of every day of my life, it was hardly surprising that my school uniform wasn't always up to scratch or that I didn't get my homework done or bring all the right stuff in. It just didn't occur to me, you see. All I thought was, well, the other boys are getting it right and I'm not, so it's my fault. And, by and large, that was reinforced by the people in charge. They told me the same thing over and over again. It's your fault, they said. So that was that. That proved it.'

He sighed. 'I know it must sound like a chronic case of feeling sorry for myself, but that was half the problem really. I never did. I didn't know you could. No-one told me. Didn't know you were allowed to. I was more puzzled than anything else. Like a chimpanzee having tea at the Ritz. I suppose any place is a jungle if no-one's taught you how to survive in it.

'Anyway, there was this one teacher we had for English. Mr Stanfield, he was called. He was a quiet man, peaceful inside sort of bloke. Gentle but strong, if you know what I mean. Wore a spotted bow-tie to school all the time. Obviously loved his subject, loved reading books and talking about books, made good jokes, and I can't remember him ever losing his cool like a few of the other teachers did. Completely different from – from anyone else I'd known. Never had a spot of trouble with his classes as far as I can remember. They liked him too much. *I* liked him. And I really wanted him to like me. I think he did in a way. I was quite good in discussions and role-plays and things like that, and, thinking back, I'd probably read more widely and indiscriminately than any of the other boys in the class, although I didn't realise it then. In fact, I actually quite looked forward to his lessons because they made me feel good sometimes, and there wasn't a lot of that feeling about, as far as I was concerned.

'The only thing was – ' he gritted his teeth – 'I never did the homework. I hardly ever did any homework for any of the subjects. And if you asked me why not I wouldn't really be able to tell you. I'd just have to give you a list of words – strain and conflict and noise and worry, words like that.'

He screwed his face up as if there was a pain right inside his head, and clawed his fingers with the frustration of not being able to express exactly what he was feeling.

'It was all so – so *scrunched* up, and so *tensed* and so *worrying*! It was like that just about all the time. All the bloody time! I became as good at finding excuses for not doing my work as some kids were at cadging money and cigarettes. I knew every angle. Talk about ducking and diving and bobbing and weaving. Not that I got away with it all the time, of course. Far from it. At my school they had a special punishment group after proper lessons had ended called the Detention Class, and I was pretty much a regular there. Really, you know, looking back, the whole thing was exhausting, but I didn't know what else to do.

'Mr Stanfield was obviously a bit puzzled about all this. I mean, he knew I enjoyed his lessons and joined in with whatever was going on, so he must have wondered why I didn't simply do the work he set the class and hand it in like all the others. Then, after two and a half terms of no homework – well, other than one scrappy piece of writing done in fifteen minutes on the bus – he must've made a decision to do something about it. Maybe he talked to the other teachers about it. I don't know.

'There was this essay, you see – on some bit of *Macbeth* I think it was – that should have been handed in weeks ago, and all he'd ever got from me was the usual series of convoluted excuses and promises that never got kept. So, one day he called me back at the end of English and said he'd got something he wanted to say to me. I can see him now, half-sitting, half-leaning on the corner of his desk at the front of the classroom, one foot swinging gently against the desk and the other on the floor. Crinkly hair, bow-tie, kind concern on his face, and some other emotion in his eyes that I didn't understand until a few moments later.

'"Simon," he said quietly and not at all crossly, "you still haven't done that Shakespeare for me, have you?"

'Sadness, that was the other thing I'd seen in his eyes. I could see that now. But it didn't make sense. What did he have to be sad about? I was the one in trouble. I automatically started in on one of my excuse and promise ploys, but he lifted a hand to stop me.

'"This is one of the saddest days of my life, Simon," he went on, still in that very quiet, very even voice, "I've been a teacher now for more than twenty years, and in all that time I have never once given any boy a detention for any offence. You are the first person I have failed with so badly that the choice has been taken away from me. I'm afraid I *must* punish you with a detention. It makes me feel very unhappy and, as I said, very, very sad."

'Then he just looked at me for a couple of seconds and said, "Is there anything you want to say to me about that?"

'I think I shook my head. Probably went a bit pale. Nothing to say on the outside. But there was a breathless, tearful little boy inside me who would have burst like a dam if anyone had ever told him how you turn your deepest, darkest feelings into words.

'I think that little boy might have said, with a very anxious little tremble in his voice, "Er, no, sir, wait a minute, excuse me, but you can't do this. I know I'm supposed to say that I'm sorry, but, you see, you don't understand. Honestly you don't. You don't understand how hard it is just to come here and stay here and keep going when things are falling apart all around you all the time at home. I don't mind you giving me a detention, Sir. You can give me three detentions or – or six detentions and I'll do them all, but please, please don't tell me I've somehow made this one of the saddest things that's ever happened to you. Please – how can I possibly have done that when every single one of my days has been taken up with making sure everything doesn't fall into a big black hole full of the worst things you can imagine turning out not to be nightmares? The thing is, there's already not enough space in my head for all the bad feelings about not being able to stop my mum and dad from fighting, sir. That's all my fault. I haven't got any room left for being the person who made this one of the saddest days of your life. I honestly haven't, Sir, and it really frightens me. Can't you just give me detentions for the rest of my life and tell me you're all right."'

As Simon looked imploringly at Gerald his eyes were swimming with tears.

'He shouldn't have done it, should he? I mean – I'm grown up now, and I know why he did it. 'Course I do. Thought it might help. He was a good man. He couldn't possibly have understood what his words did to me, but – well, he *shouldn't* have done it, should he? Sorry. Really sorry to have taken up all your time. Such a small, silly thing.'

Simon lowered his head once more and began to sob silently into the sleeves of his jacket.

'Dad, you go and round the others up,' whispered Gerald as he shifted his chair closer to the other man's, 'I'll stay and pray with Simon.'

Nodded and stood up quietly to do as he suggested. I'm very proud of my son sometimes. Glad I didn't run away to the north.

Couple of the helpers stopped me as I came out of the hall with the others tonight to mildly tell me off for one or two jokes I made about hell. Noticed a strange thing about some Christians. They seem more frightened of annoying the devil by talking frivolously about hell than they're confident of pleasing God by speaking optimistically about heaven.

Asked Gerald and the others tonight if they thought I'd got this wrong.

Thynn said, 'Well, it is possible, Adrian. You *were* wrong once. I remember it clearly. It was in nineteen-ninety-five. After thinking you'd been wrong about something it turned out that you'd actually been right, and were therefore wrong, if you see what I mean.'

The trouble with Thynn trying to be funny is that it all ends up so complicated.

I said, 'Leonard, there is one thing that you and I definitely have in common.'

'Is there? What's that, then?'

'Neither of us has the slightest idea what you're talking about.'

Quite a good discussion about hell after that. Gerald pointed out that a well-known Christian in this country had recently declared that a compassionate God could never consign anyone to everlasting torment. Instead, apparently, he'll simply annihilate the souls of the unsaved.

'Oh, well, that's all right, then, isn't it?' said Angels dismally. 'What a comfort for people to think that their souls might be annihilated by a compassionate God.'

Anne said she disagreed with what she called 'this cheerful little distortion of scripture', and reckoned everyone else ought to if they'd got any sense. Dangerous nonsense, she called it.

'What I believe,' she said, 'is that we're bound to accept that human beings who don't know Jesus – and he's the only one who's allowed to make any judgements about that – are going to find themselves separated from God, and that – well, that will be hell, won't it?'

Gerald wondered if hell would be tailored to the individual. A sort of bespoke torment.

'For instance,' he said, 'what's going to be the eternal fate of people who spend their lives compiling those long, complicated forms that I've hated and been so awful at filling in for most of my life. Just thinking about those evil, unyielding documents sends waves of crazed pessimism sweeping through my entire being. Do you all know what I mean?'

We nodded in sympathy. There can't be many people who actually enjoy filling in forms.

'Why is it,' said Anne, 'that every time I have to fill out a form in black ink, every black pen I ever owned ceases to exist precisely at that moment? How can that be? And why is it that when Adrian has to complete important forms within a couple of hours or it will be too late, he has always – *always* lost his glasses? And why do you then insist on trying to do it without your glasses, darling, when you know you're likely to discover later that you've written 'Not Sure' in the space where they want you to tell them which sex you are?'

'I have never – '

'And another thing,' interrupted Gerald, 'why is it that there's always one question demanding crucial facts that could only possibly be supplied by someone who died thirteen years ago in Samoa? And while we're on the subject, why are so many of my answers exactly half a word longer than the space they provide for them?'

'The thing I get fed up with,' said Angels, 'is finding that the most essential supporting document is invariably buried at the bottom of the last box in the final pile of rubbish in the most remote corner of the least accessible part of my loft? They do it on purpose – they must *know*!'

'I never have any trouble with forms,' said Thynn airily, 'I always got mother to fill mine in when she was alive, and Anne does them now – although she's a bit slow finding a pen sometimes.'

'So, Gerald, what sort of specially designed awfulness do you envisage for these abominable form-compilers?' asked Anne after punching Leonard.

'Well, let's have a think about it. We don't really know who's responsible for these dreadful things, do we? But whoever it is, if he's unsaved, I think I can guess what will happen when he arrives in the infernal regions. After one horror-filled glance at the lake of fire, filled with souls screaming in torment, he'll turn to the nearest mini-devil and say, 'Is there no way out of this?'

'And the mini-devil, who's been licking his lips at the prospect of this delicious question, will grin in the nastiest possible way, and hold out a gruesomely thick wad of printed paper as he replies, "Oh, yes, sir, there certainly is. Just a little, er, paperwork first. If you would care to sit down here and complete this form ... "

'The possibilities are endless, aren't they? Take the pagan traffic warden, for instance. He'll ask exactly the same question, but get a completely different answer.

'"Goodness me, yes, sir. Of course you're allowed to leave here and take up residence in heaven. In fact, we have provided a car so that you may drive yourself there. You will find it just outside the main gate with the key in the ignition."

'Filled with relief, the traffic warden will rush out through the gates of hell, only to discover that his car has been clamped – with eternal clamps!'

After a few uneasy titters and a short silence I said, 'There are times when I really thank God that I've been saved in the name of Jesus. I mean, imagine what would happen to me in Gerald's bespoke hell. I've got an awful feeling it would be even worse than what the form compilers and traffic wardens have to put up with.'

'Oh, yes, they'd have a wonderful time with you, Dad,' chuckled Gerald. 'Your personal mini-devil would gesture towards the sufferers in the lake of fire and say, "You may leave here and go straight to heaven, as soon as you manage to make a single guest of ours laugh just a tiny little bit at one of those humorous little comments of yours about the nature of heaven and hell . . ."'

'Well, anyway, the laugh is on Satan,' said Anne definitely. 'Jesus has overcome the world, and I intend to follow him into heaven. Let's hope lots of other people decide to join us. That's what this tour is all about. Anyway, I've had enough of talking about hell. Come on, Adrian, let's go to bed.

In bed tonight I told Anne about the conversation I'd had with Gerald this morning. Asked her what she thought of him going through all those difficulties and problems without letting us know what was going on.

She smiled and said, 'To be honest it doesn't surprise me in the slightest. If ever there was someone who was pretty well certain to be on the edge of all kinds of interesting disasters, it's Gerald.'

'Yes, but – '

'At the same time, I would have to say, and you would have to agree with me, that if ever there was anyone capable of finding ingenious ways out of trouble – well, that would be Gerald as well. So . . . '

'Yes, but all those things we didn't know about going on behind the scenes.' I shook my head. 'It makes you think, doesn't it?'

'Oh, well,' said Anne, 'things have always gone on behind the scenes. You've done it yourself. Do you remember when Gerald was at college and he lost all that cash – one of the disasters we did get to hear about – and you paid some money into his bank and he rang up all excited to say that he must have got his calculations all wrong because he'd got a lot more money in his account than he'd thought. You didn't tell him what you'd done, did you?'

Shook my head and sat quietly for a moment, remembering.

I said, 'Do you think God does that kind of thing?'

'How you, of all people, can ask that question is beyond me,' replied Anne sleepily. 'Why don't you read Psalm one hundred and twenty-four before you go to sleep. I seem to remember the answer's in there.' She yawned. 'In fact, you can read it out loud and then with a bit of luck we'll both go to sleep.'

Reached over for my Bible and found what I was looking for just before the end of the book of Psalms. Read the verses aloud.

'If the Lord had not been on our side – let Israel say – if the Lord had not been on our side when men attacked us, when their anger flared against us, they would have swallowed us alive; the flood would have engulfed us, the torrent would have swept over us, the raging waters would have swept us away.

'Praise be to the Lord, who has not let us be torn by their teeth. We have escaped like a bird out of the fowler's snare; the snare has been broken, and we have escaped. Our help is in the name of the Lord, the maker of heaven and earth.'

Closed my Bible and leaned over to turn out the bedside light.

Said, 'Goodnight, Anne,' but she was already fast asleep.

THURSDAY, 27 SEPTEMBER

Decided this morning to have one last go at contacting Harry Waits-Round to find out how many copies of my new book have been sold. Decided on a cunning plan. I would ask for his secretary and pretend that I was a bookshop manager who wanted to know how it was doing so that I'd know how many copies to order. Rang the publisher's office and asked to be put through to Mr Waits-Round's secretary. Phone was picked up almost immediately. To my surprise it sounded like Harry himself who answered.

'Too late!' he growled menacingly, 'you're too late. You can't get me now, and it's my dearest wish that you, if you're who I think you are, should rot in – '

'Harry, it's me, Adrian – Adrian Plass. What do you mean it's too late?'

'Adrian!' The bright sun of good humour seemed to rise once more. 'How are you? *Really* good to hear from you! Look, can't stop. Thought you

were that colleague I usually have a laugh or two with. The fact is, I've done a bit of a change around job wise. Just collecting a few bits and pieces from the office and then next week it's off to sunny Oxford to take up my new post at Napolean Weird International. Speaking of which, I know all the folks up there are really tremendous fans of yours, so we'd love to have you write for us when you get an idea for another book, so just get in touch and – '

'Harry, are you saying that you're leaving?'

'Got it in one!'

Bit disconcerted to hear this. However, decided to get just one piece of information from him before he went.

'Harry, that's great and I wish you well, I really do. Is there any chance you could tell me, while you're still there in the office, I mean, how many copies of my new book have been sold? Could you just tell me before you go?'

'Nothing I'd like to do more, my friend, but I can't,' said Harry, apparently desolated. 'The fact is, I don't have access to the old files any more. Look, tell you what, I'll put you through to the new man, fellow called Stanley Morgan. He should be able to help. And look, you keep in touch! Napolean Weird International needs writers like you. Don't tell Morgan I said that, eh? Ha-ha! See you soon, hopefully!'

'But Harry – '

Interrupted by clicks and buzzes that eventually turned into syrupy chorus music of the most ghastly variety. So vomit-makingly awful that I was about to put the phone down, when it was picked up and an angry-sounding voice with a gravelly Australian accent said, 'Okay, let me spell it out, you jumped-up son of a poisonous jellyfish. I'd rather wrestle a sixteen foot estuarine croc in a Queensland creek than swap insults with you all day, so why don't you just go and snack on a cane-toad's bladder, and when you've done that you can skin your own – '

'Er, it's me – Adrian Plass.'

Short silence. The sun must have risen for the third time that day.

'Ah, ri-i-ight! One of our leading authors. Hello! Stanley Morgan here. Call me Stan. Just taken over from the last drong-bloke. I can't tell you how much I've been looking forward to meeting you, mate! How are you going?'

'Fine, thanks. I was really only ringing to ask a question about my new book.'

'No worries, mate! Absolutely no worries. You ask away.'

'Well, I wondered if you could just tell me how many copies it's sold so far.'

When Stan replied he spoke slowly and earnestly. Even before the first two or three words emerged I had an awful feeling that I knew exactly what he was going to say.

'Adrian,' he said, 'we are *very* encouraged. Not only that, but we are proud to be able to include it on our list. And I gather that it's sold out very well … '

No time to stop for lunch today. Spotted a drive-through McDonald's and decided to get something there. As we joined the queue of cars Gerald said, 'I suppose this is the way the church will go in future.'

'What do you mean?' asked Anne.

'Well, everyone's so busy being busy nowadays that we'll probably have drive-through communion for Christians who can't spare a whole hour for worship on a Sunday.'

Angels shivered and said, 'Ugh! What a horrible thought!'

'Could happen,' said Gerald. 'Imagine it – a car pulls up with a family in it. Dad, Mum, teetotal granny and two little kids.

'"Yes, can I help you?" says the person taking the order.

'"Right," says dad, leaning out of the car window, "that'll be two large wines, one standard Ribena with extra serviettes, three breads and two small blessings please."

'"Consecrated or unconsecrated?"

'"Er, oh, consecrated, I think, please."

'"Hands laid on with the blessings or just plain?"

'"Plain's fine, thanks."

'"Nobody in your party trusting in their own righteousness?"

'"No, none of us presume."

'"Right, sir, that's two Family of God meals, consecrated, no hands, and one Weaker Brother Special with serviettes on the side. Special offer on blessings today – buy one, get one free. So, altogether that'll be a tithe of two hundred and twenty pounds and fifty pence. Pay in the plate by the exit. Just move right along to the priest at the next hatch, please. Have a nice day!"'

Rather disconcerted on arriving at this evening's venue to discover that someone, either the person who designed the posters or the one who printed them, had made what I felt to be a significant punctuation error. Just goes to show how the omission of one little comma can make all the difference. At the top of each poster the following words appeared:

ADRIAN PLASS
SPEAKER, WRITER AND
CHRISTIAN FOR ONE NIGHT ONLY

Said to Anne that I was a bit fed-up at first, but on reflection it didn't seem such a bad idea.

'You see,' I said, 'I could be a Christian, say, every Thursday evening, and do really evil, ungodly things on Friday and Saturday, then laze around from Sunday to Wednesday getting over it, and be all ready to put a lot of effort into being good on Thursday again.'

'I see,' she said, 'and, just as a matter of interest, what exactly would these evil, ungodly things be, the ones you fantasise about doing on Fridays and Saturdays?'

Felt my face reddening.

'Oh, well, you know, evil things, and, er, ungodly things . . . '

'Such as?'

'Oh – well, you know, nothing too specific. Playing fruit-machines and, er, that sort of thing.'

'Oh, right! Deadly! Very impressive. A real walk on the wild side, then?'

'Er – yes. I mean, no. I mean – I think I'd better just put the comma back where it belongs, Anne.'

'Yes,' said Anne, rather tartly, 'You just decide to put your comma back where it belongs . . . '

213

Lovely final evening at a friendly Anglican church, almost filled by two or three hundred people.

Question and answer session as part of the second section of the meeting. As it was our last night I tried to persuade Angels and Leonard to join our 'panel'. Angels flatly refused, but Leonard said he would even though he didn't know anything, had nothing to say to anyone, and would be too nervous to speak anyway. My experience is that you never know what God will say through people, whoever they are. He seems to do what he likes, on the whole. (God, I mean, not Thynn – although, now I think about it, Thynn does what he likes most of the time as well. In his case, though, it's – oh, never mind!) In any case, there's an unexpected part of Thynn that is sheer theatrical ham.

One or two of Gerald's answers are certainly worth recording.

First question, for instance, was from a lady who wanted to know what we thought about the influence of the media, and television in particular, on people who are trying to stay pure and untouched by things that might corrupt.

Gerald said, 'You're quite right, of course, it is very difficult. And the way they announce programmes doesn't make it any easier. I mean, you just imagine. There's one of your average sort of blokes sitting in front of the television, not quite sure what he's going to watch, and then this voice comes out of the telly, one of those very grown-up, responsible, gravely serious voices, and it says something like this:

'"We would like to warn viewers who may be of a nervous disposition that the following film contains scenes of an adult nature that may shock, disturb, deeply traumatise, emotionally damage or bring about lasting mental instability and illness, as well as causing those who watch it to run screaming out into the night, to vomit uncontrollably, to utterly despair of any good thing ever happening in their lives again, to weep inconsolably, to rush around with an axe indiscriminately butchering all who cross their paths, and finally to end their own lives in as painful and unpleasant a manner as possible."

'So, hearing this, our average sort of bloke's eyes light up, and he rubs his hands together and calls through to his wife, "Get some drinks and a few sandwiches going, love, there's a good film coming on!"

'I know that's a bit of an exaggeration, but we do all get tempted to indulge our appetites for things that aren't really very good for us, don't we? Let's be honest, most of us know what we can take and what we can't. If you've got a strong faith you can do just about anything without it having any effect on you, that's why Jesus was able to enjoy going to parties and eating and drinking with sinners. He was in control of himself. But if your faith is weak you'd be wise not to take too many chances. I suppose it's a matter of obedience, isn't it? God isn't going to spirit the television away so that you won't be tempted. That's why I'm always a bit worried about churches that stop their people from doing anything that even smacks of indulgence. It keeps them weak and means they can only function in tiny social spaces. That's what I think.'

Another question was about the whole Harry Potter phenomenon and the dangers for young people of getting caught up in books and films that deal with magic and the occult. Anyone who knows my son's face as well as I do would have taken his reply to this with several pinches of salt.

'Well,' said Gerald, in a voice that implied long and deep consideration of this matter in the past, 'I don't have any children of my own, but if I did, I would certainly be extremely careful to make sure that they were never exposed to people who disapprove of Harry Potter. Life is difficult enough for young people without adding to their problems. So, yes, that would certainly be a priority.'

When someone else picked up the point about how risky it is to dabble in the occult I was surprised to find myself getting quite heated on the subject.

'We always talk about dabbling in the occult,' I said, 'and I suppose dabbling means more or less the same as paddling. But why is it that we get so serious and het-up about dabbling or paddling in the occult, but hardly ever talk about having a paddle in apathy or selfishness or greed? Some of us are up to our armpits in those things. But they're more boring, aren't they? We enjoy the other stuff much more because we can stand right on the very edge of the darkness and the drama and tell ourselves that we have to be there for the very best of Christian reasons. I reckon those other things are only boring to us, though. I suspect God might find them quite interesting. The whole Bible seems to be about God trying over and over again to bring his people back to understanding that, in the end, it's love and justice and mercy that he actually wants, not just a lip-licking fascination with something we know we shouldn't touch, like children putting their fingers near a hot stove.'

Suddenly ran out of steam completely at this point and sat back feeling big and hot and stupid, embarrassed by hearing the force in my own voice. Fortunately, a rather scholarly older man with Brillo-pad hair raised his hand at that point and launched into the following question.

'On a different subject, I feel sure you would agree that Mithraic philosophy reflects, in the broadest sense, those elements of modern ideology which resist theological interpretation. And interestingly enough, as I am sure you know, the emergence of this perspective coincides with the development of retrospective studies at various institutions, and informs most dialectic approaches to Hebrew study. As we are all aware, it is therefore particularly relevant to current investigations of stylistic variations in pre-iconoclastic examples of biblical exegesis – sometimes relevant in a selectively homogeneous way, if you will excuse my little joke. My question, then, is whether, in the light of your own studies, you would agree that a schematic and purely contextual survey of New Testament passages might ultimately corroborate such a trend?'

Gerald and I looked blankly at each other, then Gerald cleared his throat and said, 'Well, good question, and definitely one for Leonard, I think.'

Thynn, despite his protestations of nervousness and knowing nothing earlier, gazed up at the ceiling, rubbing his chin with the finger and thumb of one hand as if considering the array of possible answers that were available to him.

'Mm,' he said at last, 'my colleague is quite right, the question is an extremely interesting one. I wonder if you would mind repeating it for the benefit of those who may not have understood it the first time round.'

After hearing the whole impenetrable thing again he steepled his hands under his chin and said with an air of quiet but immense authority, 'No, I would not agree.'

'Ah,' said the questioner, 'most interesting! So you would find an antithetical approach inimical to discursive forensic analysis?'

217

'Yes,' Thynn nodded solemnly, 'I would. Except, of course, in the case of – well, I think you know as well as I do.'

'Ah, yes, you mean except in the case of verbal and arhythmic catalysts, naturally,'

'Naturally,' said Thynn, sounding very slightly scornful about the learned questioner's need to actually enunciate the words.

'And you would not want to exclude the inevitable dissonance of atavistic phenomenology from your assertion?'

'N-n-no, no, no,' replied Thynn thoughtfully, as if very nearly convinced that he would not want to exclude the inevitable dissonance of atavistic phenomenology from his assertion, but not absolutely one hundred per-cent committed to the notion. 'No, I honestly don't think I would. No, I definitely wouldn't. No! No, I wouldn't *ever* want to do that.'

The questioner was amazed.

'Not even if a negatively disproportionate reductionism was involved?'

'Especially not then!' said Thynn firmly, but with a certain depth of emotion, his tone suggesting that a negatively disproportionate reductionism would have to get up pretty early in the morning to make him change his view on what to leave in and what to exclude.

'Well,' said the scholarly looking gentleman, taking his glasses off and rubbing them excitedly with a handkerchief, 'I must say that these very original insights are likely to radically affect my own view of the subject. Thank you so much for sharing the fruits of your own studies. I really am most grateful.'

'Oh, it's a pleasure,' said Thynn, 'it was nothing – absolutely nothing.'

True.

Another bit of the evening that's worth recording was a little later when we were all asked how we came to be Christians and what it meant to us. After Gerald and I had spoken, it was Leonard's turn. This time he really didn't seem to know what to say. Mumbled incoherently for a bit, then said, 'Well, I s'pose I became one because Adrian and Anne were – ones. I mean, I got to know them and just sort of thought I might as well go along with whatever they said, and it's sort of been sort of all right, I s'pose – you know ... '

As a testimony it lacked a certain something, and I could see that one or two of the people present were not very impressed. Then, almost as if it was an afterthought, Leonard began a sort of limply verbalised list that completely changed the atmosphere.

'Stopped me drinking, that was one good thing. Haven't had a drink for a long time now. Hope I never do. Belong somewhere nowadays. Made lots of new friends at church who don't seem to mind me being like I am – most of 'em anyway. Feel more safe. Don't get so frightened any more. Don't have to make as many things up as I used to.' He glanced up at the scholarly looking man and blushed a little. 'Still do sometimes. Not sure about God. As long as he doesn't turn out to be like my dad it'll be all right. Jesus is my friend. That's what they've told me. Think they're right. Hope they're right. Can't think of anything else.'

Complete silence followed by an unexpected round of applause. Leonard thought someone else must have come in and I had to explain afterwards.

The last question of the evening was from a lady who wanted to know what we thought about the Health and Wealth movement. Had to explain to some of the people there that the folk who subscribe to this movement believe that God wants to give all his followers good physical health and material prosperity, and that the only reason we don't get it is that we fail to believe and have faith in his power to do that.

Knew exactly what I thought about this ridiculous philosophy, and I was absolutely sure that Gerald would agree with me. That's what made it so difficult for me to understand the first few words he said. As he began to speak he opened the folder that lay on his lap.

'I'd like to say,' he began, 'that I understand completely where these people are coming from. Their religious philosophy makes perfect sense when you read the scriptures, and particularly a short passage in Luke and a longer one in Matthew where Jesus is giving instructions to his disciples before sending them out to preach and teach and heal. In fact,' he patted the paper on his lap, 'I brought a copy of those passages along with me just in case someone asked this very question. First of all there's the little bit from Luke. Here we are, Luke, chapter nine, verse fifty-eight. Jesus says:

'"Foxes have holes and birds of the air have nests, so it seems perfectly reasonable to me that the Son of Man and his followers should have three star accommodation at the very least while they're out on these long tiring ministry tours."

'Then we turn to Matthew, chapter ten, verses nine and ten, where Jesus says the following to his disciples:

'"Make sure you've got lots of ready cash with you, plenty of gold, silver, copper, all that sort of thing. New set of luggage wouldn't be a bad idea, and you'll need it anyway for all the clothes. You must have a regular change of tunic and, take my tip, there's no substitute for a really good range of sandals. You know, dancing sandals, casual sandals, sandals for best, sports sandals, walking-boot type sandals, they'll all come in handy at one time or another. Oh, and pop down to the shop where they sell the staffs and choose a couple each, good, sturdy, top of the range items. Be a shame to spoil the ship for a ha'p'oth of tar. Right, each of you collect a credit card from me on the way out, and – have a healthy and prosperous trip!"

'You all know I'm talking nonsense,' went on Gerald, 'at least I hope you do. The fact is that followers of Jesus over the years have learned that one of their top priorities is to trust God whatever their circumstances happen to be. Whether we're ill or well, whether we're rich or poor, we trust that the very best is happening for us, and we thank God that our souls are tucked away safely in the palm of his hand.'

He picked up a Bible from the floor beside his seat.

'And just to finish my answer to your question, here's a real quote from the Bible. It's Saint Paul writing to the Corinthians. Now, if ever there was someone who should have been able to take advantage of this health and wealth stuff it's Paul. But you listen to this:

'"Are they Hebrews? So am I. Are they Abraham's descendants? So am I. Are they servants of Christ? (I am out of my mind to talk like this.) I am more. I have worked much harder, been in prison more frequently, been flogged more severely, and been exposed to death again and again. Five times I received from the Jews the forty lashes minus one. Three times I was beaten with rods, once I was stoned, three times I was shipwrecked, I spent a night and a day in the open sea, I have been constantly on the move. I have been in danger from rivers, in danger from bandits, in danger from my own country-men, in danger from Gentiles; in danger in the city, in danger in the country, in danger at sea; and in danger from false brothers. I have laboured and toiled and often gone without sleep; I have known hunger and thirst and have often gone without food; I have been cold and naked. Besides everything else, I face daily the pressure of my concern for all the churches. Who is weak, and I do not feel weak? Who is led into sin, and I do not inwardly burn? If I must boast, I will boast of the things that show my weakness."

'I hope that's helped to answer your question,' said Gerald.

I got the distinct impression that it had.

Sold another two of Zak's water-colours this evening, and one went last night, so that's four altogether in the second half of the tour. Really looking forward to seeing Bernadette's face when I next visit her.

Gerald put Barry out of his misery on the way back in the van tonight over the 'Jesus deliberately saying something untrue' thing. Began when Barry said, with a hideously poor attempt at sounding casual and unconcerned, 'Oh, Gerald, I just wanted to say that I realise now that the whole thing about the Lord not telling the truth was simply a – a joke aimed at me. I see now how amusing it was. Ha – ha! Silly me! I should have known that there was no such verse.'

Barry looked imploringly at the back of Gerald's head, but Gerald, who was sitting next to me in the passenger seat, just shook his head and turned to look at the Bible expert very seriously.

'Not a joke, Barry,' he said. 'Still not got it, then?'

Barry almost whimpered.

Anne leaned over from behind my seat and smacked Gerald lightly on the top of his head.

'Put us all out of our misery, will you, son of mine? I'm beginning to think Barry's right and you made it all up yourself.'

'Oh, all right, Mumsy, if you say so. Right! Barry, who is the greatest man ever to have been born?'

'Er, the Lord Jesus, of course. Yes, without doubt.'

'And he was definitely born of woman, was he not?'

'Yes, yes, his father was God, but his mother was Mary.'

'Right. Now let's talk about John the Baptist.'

'John the Baptist?'

'Yes, the cousin of Jesus. Tell me, Barry, according to Matthew, what did Jesus say to the crowds about John after answering the question about whether he was the Messiah or not?'

'Ah, well, he asked them what they went out into the desert to see, and he went on to say that – '

'No, a little bit after that, in the eleventh verse of the eleventh chapter to be precise. You read out what it says.'

In a whirr of page-turning Barry found the place and began to read.

'"I tell you the truth: among those born of women there has not risen anyone greater than John the Baptist – " Ah, I see what you mean.'

'There you are,' said Gerald, 'it was very nice of Jesus, and I'm sure he had a particular reason for saying it, but it wasn't true, was it?'

Poor Barry was less than graceful in defeat.

'Mm, yes, I er – I'll need to check translations . . . '

The others may have found my joke about the contortionist chicken a bit of a shock, but no-one could have been more surprised than we all were when Barry decided that it was his turn to do a 'someone at the door' joke when we got back to the hotel. Despite living in a different religious universe from the rest of us, there has definitely been a sort of sadness in him as we've got nearer to the end of the tour. Anne says that, although we might not be particularly impressive as human beings or Christians, there is a kind of warm togetherness about our little group that she thinks Barry has probably never experienced. Perhaps, she said, inside himself he's longing to be part of it. Typical of Anne to be so understanding about someone who has infuriated her so much.

Up to now Gerald's sense of humour and the kinds of things we laugh at in general have left Barry puzzled and vaguely worried. Apart from anything else, I suppose he hasn't been able to find a verse in scripture to confirm its value, not as far as he can see, anyway. Bearing this in mind, working out one of these jokes and actually doing it must have been a sort of *Raiders of the Lost Ark* adventure for him. At first we didn't even realise that it was meant to be a joke. We were all sitting in the little bar-cum-sitting-room of our final hotel, enjoying the fact that the tour had happened and been relatively successful, and relaxing before going to bed with drinks and a bag of wonderful, softly plump jam doughnuts bought earlier by Angels, when

Barry came in and stood just inside the door, shifting from foot to foot and looking very nervous.

Gerald said, 'Come and take a seat, Barry, we're just winding down, getting drunk, uttering a profanity or two, planning a few juicy sins, that sort of thing.'

Barry smiled a twitchy little smile in recognition of the fact that he had begun to understand that comments like this from my son were deliberately flippant and provocative.

'Er, I will come and sit down in a moment,' he said, 'but before I do that, I just wanted to tell you that there's a – a very troubled gentleman in reception who was at the meeting tonight and he's wondering if it would be all right for him to ask an important question.'

'Here am I, Lord, send Gerald,' was my first, basely ignoble thought. The last thing I felt like doing was sitting down with someone who needed to talk on and on into the early hours of the morning about the state of his soul, when I could have had another drink and, if I played my cards right, at least half of Anne's second doughnut, before flopping into bed for the night. Repented almost immediately, sighed, and started to lever myself out of my chair.

'The thing is,' went on Barry, 'he has nowhere to stay for the night and he was wondering if we could help. He's called Mr Beach, by the way.'

Even then none of us twigged for a moment or two. I thought it must be someone who was hoping we'd stump up the price of a bed for the night. I don't know what the others thought. It was Angels who suddenly realised what was going on.

'I think it might be a joke,' she said, narrowing her eyes speculatively in Barry's direction. 'Yes, I do believe it is.'

I relaxed back into my chair. What a relief! What a surprise! I think everyone was amazed.

'So,' said Gerald, clasping his hands together and resting his chin on the ends of his two forefingers, 'what kind of accommodation would he be looking for, then, this Mr Beach?'

Barry cleared his throat uneasily.

'Oh, just something to tide him over,' he said hoarsely.

Barry must have been extremely gratified by the reaction that his joke received. Perhaps we went slightly over the top in our loud appreciation. Thynn certainly did. He produced ridiculously loud and unconvincing guffaws of wild mirth. Still, he meant well, and Barry seemed pleased. I privately didn't think his Beach could hold a candle to my chicken, but we wanted to encourage him, and he certainly seemed to enjoy being accepted in a different sort of way. It was rather nice.

Long, sleepy, doughnut-filled discussion after that about such trivial subjects as dying and going to heaven and what we all thought it would be like.

Rather pleased to find my personal vision of heaven, arriving at some Indian restaurant in the late evening after giving a talk somewhere and lifting that first glass of Kingfisher lager to my lips, was received by the group with the right kind of nodding, reverential silence. Heaven would have to go some to match that, they seemed to feel.

Gerald said he supposed that if we were right about hell being tailored to individuals, then heaven might have to be just the same.

'In which case,' he said, 'there'll have to be a special place set aside for Pharisees to leave their cars, won't there?'

I did think about having a stab at guessing, but it felt too much like hard work.

'All right, come on, then, Gerald,' smiled Anne, 'you obviously want to tell us. What will they call the special place that's set aside for Pharisees to leave their cars?'

'The Pray and Display Car-park, of course.'

Groans.

'And what about you, Barry,' asked Angels, 'what would heaven be like if it was specially designed for you?'

Barry seemed to be in an unusually relaxed, mellow mood after his first successful foray into the world of humour. He leaned back in his chair, staring at the ceiling and thinking.

'Well,' he said at last, 'leaving God out of the picture for a moment, I would love heaven to be like one of those beautiful early summer mornings when I get up before anyone else and walk the dogs and just enjoy being in the middle of nature all on my own.'

There was an expression of utter rapture on his face as he went on.

'The colours and the freshness and the feeling of peace. If it could be like that, only going on and on – well, it would be wonderful.'

Then, abruptly, perhaps suddenly becoming aware of his own voice, his face changed. No more rapture. No more relaxation. He was like a child sitting up straight in his seat and paying attention to the teacher instead of gazing dreamily through the window on a Friday afternoon.

'Of course,' he continued, in dutiful tones, 'in fact we know that it's the love of God that draws us, and because of that perfect love we cannot help but be blissfully happy because of his promises to us in the scriptures.'

No-one said anything for a little while after that, and then I happened to glance over at Gerald. To my surprise he seemed to be using a tissue to wipe the tears from his eyes. Anne must have noticed at the same moment.

'You all right, Gerald?' she asked.

He took a second or two before answering.

'I suppose I suddenly felt – I dunno – sad and confused about what Barry said. Did you notice what happened? With God "out of the picture" everything shone. As soon as he allowed God back in all the joy had gone. It was as if he suddenly remembered that he might have come close to giving the wrong answer to some divine exam question, and he was worried he might have lost his chance of "getting in" when judgement time comes.'

He turned and spoke directly to Barry, not at all aggressively, but with a sort of passionate entreaty.

'Don't you see, Barry,' he said, 'that you're not being fair on God? Do you honestly think that he doesn't enjoy strolling through an early summer morning as much as you do? Has it not occurred to you that he might be really hurt by the fact that you don't want him there with you when you're in the middle of relishing all the colours and the freshness? Why on earth or in heaven or anywhere else you like would you not want him beside you on one of the few occasions when you truly experience joy? He made those things you love, didn't he? What is the matter with us Christians, that we shove one load of excellent things into the "not God" section of our lives, and the rubbishy rest into some strange, abstract little corral made of words and fear and lack of trust in the value of real things? God made everything that's beautiful and fine, and those things don't lose their worth because they haven't got themselves slotted into some form of words or piece of ritual that we've allowed to grow way beyond its real importance.'

I caught Anne's eye. This was Gerald as neither of us had ever known him before. And he wasn't finished yet. He was addressing everybody now.

'Just think about it – a plump little Welsh poet, a womaniser and an alcoholic, produces some of the most heartwrenchingly beautiful arrangements of words that the world will ever hear or see, and we get worried because his morality didn't match his creativity. Well, let me tell you it's hard luck. The beauty and the inventiveness came from God, whatever anyone thinks of the channel. And who are you and I to judge, anyway? I call myself a Christian, but I doubt if I shall ever produce anything a twentieth as beautiful as the things that came from that man's pen.'

He paused for a moment, gazing out of the window at the handful of stars visible in a cloudy night sky. He continued in a much softer voice.

'Have you ever seen a secular sunset? Far less dramatic and colourful than a Christian one, of course. Or a gay rainbow? All the same colours but in a different order from the one we're used to. What about an adulterous eclipse of the sun? Tinged with treachery and disappointment, perhaps? No, I don't think so, do you? Wherever you look from and whoever you are, they're always the same. Let's try not be silly. You turn one of your dogs backwards and take him for a walk with you in the mornings, Barry. I've got a feeling you'll enjoy it even more.

After all, Jesus always wanted to be where people were, not where someone else thought they or he ought to be.' He blinked suddenly as if coming to. 'Sorry to go on.'

'I suppose,' said Anne, 'that in a way we've got just as many false Gods nowadays as the old Israelites had in the Bible. But when you think about it ours are probably more sneaky and dangerous, because they're actually disguised as the real God. Some of them have even got his name.' She shivered suddenly. 'It's a horrible thought. It's like Gerald says. What they want most is to keep us away from places where you find things like life and love and laughter and beauty and tears and disaster. Those are all real, vulgar, human things, but wherever you find them I reckon you're going to find God.' She looked round at us all with a hint of surprise on her face, as if an old under-standing had unexpectedly sunk in a little deeper. 'He really did become man, didn't he?'

'They're right, you know, Barry,' said Angels from the depths of her chair, 'I don't know anything about it, but I'm beginning to realise you can't leave God out of the picture – not even for a moment.'

Barry didn't react very much to any of this. Just sat very still, looking a little shell-shocked. Every now and then he nodded very gently to himself.

Mood completely changed a few minutes after that when Anne asked me if I'd thought about whether I wanted to be buried or cremated. When I said that, all things considered, I thought I'd prefer cremation, Gerald offered to put his coat on and take me down there now to save time.

Finally asked Angels how she felt about dying and going to heaven and all that.

She said, 'Well, I have to be honest and say that, just at the moment, I'm so excited about finding something and someone to be alive for that I haven't really given much thought to heaven.'

'What would you like to be written on your gravestone?' asked Gerald.

She said, 'I suppose Leonard and I will be in the same grave if everything works out and we – you know – get married and everything, but, well, let me think.'

She glanced at me and smiled that new relaxed smile that we are all beginning to like so much.

'Yes, I think I've got it. If I were to be buried on my own, which I honestly hope I won't be, I'd like there to be a nice, smooth flat slab of marble laid over the top of my grave, and on the actual gravestone I'd like it to say something along the lines of – just a moment . . .'

She took a pad of paper from her bag, wrote on it for a minute or two, then held it up for us all to see. It said:

HERE BENEATH A MARBLE SLAB

I WAIT FOR HEAVENLY BLISS

THE PLACES WHERE THEY MADE ME DANCE

WERE HALF THE SIZE OF THIS

Our laughter was interrupted by one of those statements from Thynn that make you think you must have unwittingly taken a wrong turn in the universe.

He said, 'If I end up buried on my own I'd like the gravestone to say, "Men walked under his huge legs and peeped about looking for somewhere to be buried". That's what I've always wanted since I was about thirteen.'

Profound silence.

Finally Gerald said, 'Leonard, I'm going to ask this question, not because I seriously expect there to be a rational explanation, but because there is a certain, almost – yes, a narcotic pleasure in being lifted up and out into the shockingly surreal world of your thinking processes.'

'Well, it's very nice of you to say so,' said Thynn, 'please feel free to ask anything you wish.'

'Thank you, Leonard.'

'Not at all, Gerald.'

'Right, bearing in mind that, as far as I know, you have more or less average sized legs, why should anyone be walking under them, and why would these men who weren't able to walk under them be looking for somewhere to be buried, and, most curious of all, why would you want huge legs anyway, and what made you say any of those things in the first place?'

'Act one, scene two,' said Angels unexpectedly. 'Correct me if I'm wrong, Leonard, but I think you probably went to see a production of Julius Caesar when you were thirteen. Am I right?'

Leonard was amazed.

'Yes, I think that's right. Well, you're right, it was in a play, although I could never remember afterwards what the play was called. I just remember there was this bit about a famous person and what a great man he was, and it always stuck in my mind and made me think that I'd like them to say I had huge legs and that sort of thing after I died. Fancy you knowing that, Angels.'

'I always loved Shakespeare,' said Angels. She quoted softly: '"Why man, he doth bestride the narrow world like a Colossus, and we petty men walk under his huge legs, and peep about to find ourselves dishonourable graves." We'll look it up when we get home, Leonard, and you can read it for yourself.'

If Leonard was a slave to his new girlfriend before, he's an even more devoted one now.

When we got to bed at last I wrote up my diary then showed Anne the entry for today, right up to the bit about Angels and her gravestone and Leonard and his.

She read it, chuckling every now and then, and finally she said, 'That's really good, darling. You have worked hard on this thing, haven't you?'

'Tried,' I said modestly.

'Wouldn't it be puzzling for future generations,' she said, tilting her head on one side, 'if the whole of today's entry was destroyed by fire or something, except for the one line that they would never, ever be able to understand?'

'Which one would that be, then? It's all quite clear as far as I can recall.'

She smiled.

'I'll read it out. Just a minute – yes, here we are, this is the bit. "I privately didn't think his Beach could hold a candle to my chicken."'

She thought for a moment, then tapped the page.

'You know, entirely meaningless as those words would be to anyone who didn't know the rest of the story . . . '

'Yes?'

'They are very much you, darling.'

We both laughed.

'Have you enjoyed the tour, Anne?'

'Oh, yes!' she said. 'It's been *so* lovely to have Gerald back with us for a little while, just like the old days but so much more grown up in so many ways. And I really do have high hopes for Leonard and Angels. She's a darling, full of pain, but a real darling. I think God has put them together to help with the business of mending each other. Even starchy old Barry doesn't seem quite as ghastly now as he did when we started. Most of all, though, sweetheart, it's been good for you and me to be together doing something even slightly useful, hasn't it? I've loved that. Have you?'

'Oh, yes,' I said, 'I've loved that too.'

AFTER THE TOUR

So, those were the highlights from my diary of our tour, and I do hope Anne was right in thinking that other people will find some interest in the happenings of those seven days.

We all had very mixed feelings about coming back on the day after our final evening. It's always nice to get home, so cosy and right, but when you go away in a group like that a whole other little world is created, and it seems such a shame that it may never happen quite like that again. Anne and I spent a morning with Zak's widow on the Saturday of the following weekend. Bernadette insisted on hearing every detail of the tour, almost as though Zak had actually come along with us, and she was being told how he had 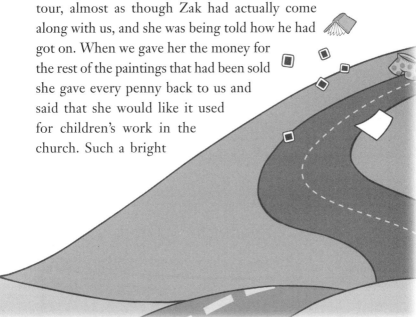 got on. When we gave her the money for the rest of the paintings that had been sold she gave every penny back to us and said that she would like it used for children's work in the church. Such a bright and good lady, and so sad without her Zak. We must keep in touch.

As a matter of detail, the final cost of the whole thing came to thirty or forty pounds more than we ended up with when we added the money from ticket sales to one or two large, quite unexpected and very welcome gifts from various people in the church.

Thynn made the foolish suggestion that we ought to add the shortfall out of our own pockets so that we could tell everybody how wonderfully exact the Lord's provision was. Anne got a bit cross with him over that, and said that God had provided quite enough in all sorts of ways without us having to 'cook the books' in order to make him look better. Leonard repented and said he agreed, but I know he still thought it was a brilliantly good idea.

Barry certainly didn't seem to mind making up the difference. As he said himself, he had been expecting his contribution to run into hundreds. When I asked him how he felt about the tour overall, he looked very thoughtful for a moment, then he said, 'I do begin to feel that there may be a case for, as it were, allowing the sentient aspects of life to run a parallel course with more solidly theological considerations.'

I think he meant he was beginning to discover that it was all right to feel things. I hope that is what he meant. I think it would probably make him much happier. Incidentally, one interesting consequence of our tour is that Barry has visited on at least two occasions since we returned, to ask for Anne's advice. Amazing! When I think how soundly she told him off on one or two occasions while we were away I find that quite remarkable. Perhaps it's because he knows Anne will always say exactly what she thinks and be nice to him as soon as it's actually possible.

A thought has just occurred to me. If he falls in love with her like Henry Rung did, and I die, and he marries Anne, then Barry would become Gerald's Step Ingstone. Hmm, I don't think I'll let Gerald see that joke.

Leonard and Angels are still going strong, and the good news is that both of them have managed to get jobs in the very store where they've been going to watch videos. Angels is working on the checkout counters, saying 'Hello!' brightly to each customer and ringing a little bell to call her supervisor for a quite bewildering variety of reasons. Angels is very funny talking about her job. She seems so much more relaxed now, serious about her new faith and very keen to learn all she can about being a follower of Jesus. She still dances for the old folk at Clay House from time to time, and she says that, assuming anyone wanted her to, she might do something in our church when the right time comes. We see a lot of her in the evenings and at weekends, and we really are becoming very fond of her. It's a bit like having a daughter – I should imagine.

Leonard's job is quite different. He's one of that very particular and necessary race of men who tramp around the car-parks and the immediate neighbourhood in all weathers, collecting abandoned shopping trolleys and joining them together in great long chains so that they can be pushed back to the shop. He says that he always did want to be an engine driver, and this is the nearest he's ever likely to get to it. When Gerald came down the other weekend and heard that these two 'young' lovers were working in the supermarket, he asked Leonard very gravely whether or not the store had a special check-out counter for Anglican vicars and curates.

'No,' said Leonard blankly, 'I don't think so.'

Gerald looked surprised.

'Well, our local supermarket does,' he said. 'I use it all the time. There's a sign over the counter saying "CHURCH OF ENGLAND CLERGYMEN ONLY : THIRTY-NINE ARTICLES OR LESS".'

'Oh,' replied Thynn casually, as if this was a totally feasible proposition, 'no, we don't have one of those, but we do have a checkout where people sometimes get healed.'

Gerald's eyebrows shot up.

'You do?'

'Yes, it's a specially wide exit, and there's a notice saying that it's for the use of disabled customers only, and it's never ever as busy as the other counters. I've often seen people limping quite badly as they come up to pay for their shopping, and then, as soon as they've gone past the customer service desk and got round the corner to where the newspapers are, they're suddenly healed.'

'Ah,' said Gerald, 'Yes, I think I see . . .'

Leonard and Angels are saving hard for their marriage. Leonard inherited the house he lives in from his mother, so that will be all right, but apart from that they haven't got two pennies to rub together. One way or another it will be okay, though. My only niggling worry has been whether Angels will go on wanting Leonard as her life starts to come back together and she gets in touch with the grown-up who's been hiding away inside her for so long. Losing her might destroy Leonard. Asked Anne what she thought.

She said, 'First of all, darling, it's not really any of our business. God and Leonard and Angels have to sort all that out between them, and, of course, if there is anything we can do to help, we'll do it like a shot, won't we? But if you're asking my opinion – well, I think they're a fixture. It's a long road back for Angels, and I think she's decided that Leonard is the one she wants to travel with. She needs to be safe. I reckon they'll be okay.'

I do pray that Anne's right.

As far as we can tell, Gerald seems to be going from strength to strength in his parish, although he did tell us about one unfortunate incident. He went round to visit an elderly couple called Mr and Mrs Jenkins one afternoon, and after staying for half an hour or so was asked by the lady of the house if he would like to stay for some ham and salad.

'Oh, no,' said Gerald politely, 'thanks ever so much, but you weren't expecting me so you probably won't have enough. I'll eat at home.'

Mrs Jenkins, the sort of woman who says she can't come on Wednesday because 'that's when I do my voluntary work', pressed and pressed, insisting that there was plenty of ham, until Gerald's resistance was finally worn down, and he did accept the invitation. Mr Jenkins just looked on gloomily and said nothing. Gerald's plate of ham and salad was duly served up at the dining-room table, and he had just begun to make his way through it when he realised that neither Mr or Mrs Jenkins was actually having anything. Both were sitting at the opposite side of the table, staring expressionlessly at him as he consumed ham.

Gerald stopped in mid-chew.

'Er, are you not joining me?' he enquired rather nervously.

'No,' said Mrs Jenkins with a sort of melancholy relish, 'that's our tea you're eating.'

Gerald is rarely at a loss, but he said that this hair-raising experience left him speechless, especially as his mouth was still half-full of the ham that his host and hostess had so graciously sacrificed in order that the young curate might eat.

We do miss Gerald an awful lot, but he does come down every other week or so, and just recently he let slip the fascinating fact that there may be a 'significant other' in the offing. Can't wait to meet whoever it is. I do hope she turns out to be just a tad less forceful and aggressive than Elsie Burlesford, who was Gerald's girlfriend for a while when he was living here at home. We shall have to wait and see.

I said to Anne last night, 'Wouldn't it be fun to do another tour next year, and have Gerald and, er ... '

'The significant other?' supplied Anne.

'Yes, wouldn't it be good to all go off together? Leonard and Angels and you and me and Gerald and ... '

'Thingy.'

'Gerald and Thingy and Barry if he puts the money up again.'

'Adrian!'

'It would be fun to do it again, though, wouldn't it, Anne?'

'Yes,' said Anne, 'it would.'

And Jesus Will Be Born
A Collection of Christmas Poems, Stories and Reflections

Adrian Plass

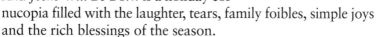

In this gentle and humorous anthology of poems, stories, commentary and reflections, Adrian Plass invites us to celebrate Christmas in its many facets. *And Jesus Will Be Born* is a holiday cornucopia filled with the laughter, tears, family foibles, simple joys and the rich blessings of the season.

Setting the poignant, the madcap, the joyous and the tender in artful counterpoint, this is a book to be savoured over the entire holiday season. It offers something for everyone in every setting – family readings, personal libraries and even church pulpits.

And Jesus Will Be Born speaks to the full spectrum of our humanity, celebrating the golden Christmas traditions, poking playfully at our seasonal foibles, observing our less-than-noble attitudes with an eye that is at once honest and gracious – and always looking towards the Person around whom all that is truly Christmas revolves.

In the midst of our festivities, Adrian Plass gently reminds us why we need a Saviour. And he points us towards the unfathomable possibilities that have been opened to us, and the joy and hope that are ours, because Jesus was born long ago in Bethlehem and is born today in us.

Hardcover: 0-007-13051-1   Softcover: 0-007-13052-X

Pick up a copy today at your favourite bookshop!

ZONDERVAN™

GRAND RAPIDS, MICHIGAN 49530 USA

WWW.ZONDERVAN.COM

The Heart of the Family

**Laughter and Tears
from a Real Family**

Adrian Plass

Families are funny. They can be sheer heaven or they can be – well, less than heavenly. One thing is for sure, though. The happiest of family members will readily concede that tears are as essential as laughter if we are to survive the dramatic peaks and troughs of close human interaction. This is no less true when love is unconditional and there is a real generosity of spirit in those concerned.

Through fiction and fact, poetry and prose, this book opens the lid of family life and invites the reader to explore the richly varied and entertaining events and characters that he or she will discover there. This collection of homely treasures will certainly make us smile, and there is a very good chance that some of them will make us cry.

As you will see in the course of this book, this is as true in the family of the church as it is anywhere else. The heart of the family is love, and at the heart of love you will find God.

Hardcover: 0-007-13047-3   Softcover: 0-007-13048-1

Pick up a copy today at your favourite bookshop!

ZONDERVAN™

GRAND RAPIDS, MICHIGAN 49530 USA

WWW.ZONDERVAN.COM

Ghosts
The Story of a Reunion

Adrian Plass

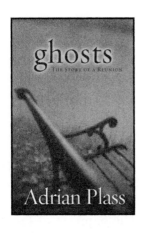

The strangest things happen when friends are reunited after twenty years apart. When together last, the friends were members of the same youth group and – on the whole – had life to look forward to. Now middle-aged, some are still optimistic but others are worn-out and weary. One has lost his faith, and another is struggling to reconcile the promises of his Christian beliefs with the recent death of his wife.

When reunited for a weekend away, the friends find themselves in Headly Manor, reputed to be one of the most haunted houses in England. What does it mean to stay in a haunted house? Strangely warm beds on cold days, objects unaccountably moving from room to room, and little girls in old-fashioned clothes seen walking across the lawn? Or something more subtle, but potentially much more frightening?

This engaging story blends Adrian Plass's rich style of humour with his knack for addressing the deep issues we all face, such as faith, grief, love, fear – and most crippling of all afflictions, the fear of fear.

Softcover: 0-551-03110-7   Unabridged Audio Pages® CD: 0-310-25215-6

ZONDERVAN™

GRAND RAPIDS, MICHIGAN 49530 USA

WWW.ZONDERVAN.COM

Never Mind the Reversing Ducks

A Non-Theologian Encounters Jesus in the Gospel According to St Mark

Adrian Plass

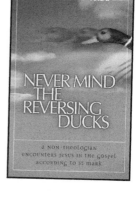

This book is a chatty, quirky, serious, tragic and humourous look at the gospel of Mark. In Adrian Plass's inimitable style, it brings the reader encouraging comment, funny stories, and profound truth. The full text of Mark's gospel is included and is broken into ninety sections. Each portion of Scripture is followed by Adrian's comment and a prayer.

Plass brings his own unique perspective to this meditation on Mark. An adventurous, challenging, witty and often poignant look at the events in the life of Jesus, *Never Mind the Reversing Ducks* addresses the deep issues we all face.

Hardcover: 0-007-13043-0

Softcover: 0-007-13044-9

From Growing Up Pains to the Sacred Diary

Nothing Is Wasted

Adrian Plass

Adrian Plass has a way of telling our stories by telling his, and by so doing has endeared himself to a multitude of readers. Perhaps his secret lies in his humour, from the dark to the absurd. Or it could be his penchant for poking gently but frankly at the foibles of Christian living. Both qualities are on display here, with two of Plass's best-loved books rolled into one.

The Growing Up Pains of Adrian Plass offers reflections on a difficult passage in the author's personal journey, during which the television programme Company and some of its memorable guests made a deep impact on Plass's faith. The *Sacred Diary of Adrian Plass Aged 37 1/2* is a laugh-filled, fictional daily chronicle of family and church exploits, featuring Plass's literary alter ego and a memorable cast of supporting characters.

Softcover: 0-310-27857-0

Pick up a copy today at your favourite bookshop!

ZONDERVAN™

GRAND RAPIDS, MICHIGAN 49530 USA

WWW.ZONDERVAN.COM

Nothing but the Truth
A Collection of Short Stories and Parables

Adrian Plass

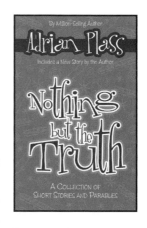

A parable can 'entertain at the front door while the truth slips in through a side window,' and few Christian writers can tell one as deftly as Adrian Plass. In this collection of short stories he is thought-provoking, inventive and easily able to traverse that short distance between a smile and a tear.

Combining material from *Father to the Man* and *The Final Boundary* and introducing a fresh new story, *Nothing but the Truth* reveals the more serious side of Adrian Plass. Seasoned with his trademark humour, the stories portray characters responding to emotional or spiritual crises – and in so doing, reveal truths about ourselves, the games we sometimes play and the love we all are searching for.

Softcover: 0-310-27859-7

Pick up a copy today at your favourite bookshop!

We want to hear from you. Please send your comments about this book to us in care of zreview@zondervan.com. Thank you.

GRAND RAPIDS, MICHIGAN 49530 USA

WWW.ZONDERVAN.COM